轻 松 学 谚 语
Easy Way to Learn Chinese
Proverbs

编 著: 李庆军 丁华

Compiled by

Li Qingjun and Ding Hua

Love Githa

York

3rd July. 2008

新 世 界 出 版 社
NEW WORLD PRESS

First Edition 1998
Second Printing 1998
Idea Created by Jiang Hanzhong
Edited by Song He
Illustrations by Liu Yang
Book Design by Li Hui

ISBN 7-80005-374-1

Published by
NEW WORLD PRESS
24 Baiwanzhuang Road, Beijing 100037, China

Distributed by
NEW WORLD PRESS
24 Baiwanzhuang Road, Beijing 100037, China
Tel: 0086-10-68326645
Fax: 0086-10-68326679

Printed in the People s Republic of China

前言

　　谚语，是中国古代灿烂文明的产物，在现代汉语中仍起着积极的作用，已经成了现代汉语中不可缺少的重要组成部分。谚语形式简炼，寓意深刻，具有很强的表现力。

　　近年来，中国与外界的交往日益频繁，越来越多的外国人来到中国生活、工作。一方面，外国人迫切希望了解中国的历史、文化以及语言文字；另一方面，中国人在与外国朋友交谈中，经常遇到这样的问题：有些汉语中的习惯表达法，包括谚语，很难准确、恰当地译成英语，于是就产生了交流的障碍。

　　本书正是为解决上述问题而编写的。编者精选了现代汉语中常用的八十三条谚语，中英文相对照，以故事的形式，详尽地说明了它们的来历、涵义和用法。一些故事还配有生动形象的插图，以帮助读者理解和记忆。

　　对于那些正在学习汉语，或是对中国文化感兴趣的外国人来说，本书就象一幅长卷，向他们展示着中国悠久的历史和灿烂的文明，令他们在轻松的欣赏之余，领略中国文化的魅力，同时丰富其汉语语汇，提高其中文的语言和文字表达能力。

　　书中的译文经外国专家润色，准确、流畅、生动、优美。因而，对于中国读者来说，本书可以作为英语学习的辅助读物。通过阅读译文，读者不仅可以掌握谚语的英译法，更可以从中领略到纯正、地道的英文表达法，从而提高英语口语和书面表达能力，以便于更加自如地与外国朋友进行交流。

FOREWORD

Chinese proverbs, which epitomize Chinese history and culture, are a treasure of Chinese language.

In recent years, with the cultural and economic exchanges between China and the outside world becoming increasingly frequent, more and more foreigners have come to China for travelling or working. On the one hand, foreigners thirst for gaining knowledge about Chinese history and culture and learning Chinese language; on the other hand, some Chinese people find it difficult to translate the Chinese proverbs properly into English when they talk with foreign friends.

This book has been compiled to solve the aforementioned problem. It consists of eighty-three proverbs with one story (both in Chinese and English) following each. They are the most popular ones in modern Chinese usage. To enhance comprehension by foreign readers, each proverb in this book appears in two forms: Chinese characters and *pinyin*. With the vivid illustrations matching some of the stories, readers will get a strong impression and a distinct idea of the proverbs.

In addition to displaying a panorama of ancient China and offering much knowledge concerning Chinese history, this book provides foreign readers with a chance to become acquainted with the essence of the Chinese language. By reading this book and trying to apply the proverbs in writing or everyday conversation, foreign readers will find their Chinese friends amazed and impressed, and thus will become more confident in the study of the Chinese language.

Furthermore, the English translation of this book has been proofread by Thomas Shou, an American expert who is proficient in the Chinese language, and thus it presents fluent and elegant English to readers. Therefore, it can help Chinese readers to improve their spoken and written English, enabling them to communicate with foreign friends more freely.

目录
CONTENTS

一 人 得 道　鸡 犬 升 天

yì　rén　dé　dào　　jī　quǎn　shēng　tiān

When one man finds the Tao, even his chickens and dogs ascend to heaven with him

传说汉代淮南王刘安崇信神仙道术，一心幻想修炼成仙。他不惜花重金招致天下道术之士，让他们探求得道成仙的途径。这事被住在天上的八位仙翁知道了，便一起来到刘安家中，将炼制仙丹的秘术传授给他。经过几年功夫，刘安终于炼成了仙丹。

　　就在这时，有人告发他图谋反叛，皇帝派兵捉拿他。刘安赶忙去见仙翁，把这事告诉他们。仙翁们说："这正是上帝让你升天成仙呢！如果你不遭遇这个灾祸，会长久迷恋人间荣华，日复一日，你是不愿意离开人世间的。现在可以服用仙丹了。"刘安要求让他的亲戚好友和他一道升天成仙，仙翁也答应了。于是刘安把亲友们请来，打开炼丹炉，顿时香气四溢。每人分食了几粒仙丹后，个个都飘然升上天去。刘安家中的鸡狗，闻得仙丹的香气，都跑到炼丹炉前，不住地舐啄炉中剩下的药渣，结果鸡狗也跟着腾飞而去。

　　根据这个故事，后人概括出"一人得道，鸡犬升天"的谚语，用来形容一个人做官得势后，同他有关系的人也跟着飞黄腾达起来。

In the Han Dynasty (206 B.C.-220 A.D.), there is a legend about a nobleman from Huainan named Liu An who was a devout believer in Taoist magic. His one dream in life was to become an immortal. He spared no amount of money to hire the best Taoist masters in the land to help him find the path of immortality. When the eight immortals in the heavens knew about this, they made a special visit to Liu's home. There they passed on to Liu the secret of refining the elixir of immortality. After many years of hard work, Liu finally created the elixir of immortality.

It was just at this time he was accused of political conspiracy and was arrested by the emperor. Liu immediately sought the ancient immortals and explained his case to them. The ancient immortals replied, "This is just God's way of preparing you to ascend heaven and become an immortal! If you never faced such a calamity in your life, your heart would forever be drawn to the glory and splendor of this world. And with the passing of time, soon you will no longer even desire to leave this human world behind. Now is the time for you to take the elixir." Liu An then requested that all his relatives and good friends could also go up with him and become immortals. The ancient immortals agreed, and so Liu An invited his family and good friends over and then opened up the furnace refining the elixir. Immediately the aroma of the elixir filled the room. After taking a few grams of the elixir, they all ascended one by one towards the heavens. When the chickens and dogs of the Liu An's household caught a whiff of the aroma, they also came running over to the furnace to lick up or peck at all the medicinal residue in the furnace. As a result, even the chickens and dogs ascended with the rest towards heaven.

This story was later summarized into the proverb "when one man finds the Tao, even his chickens and dogs ascend to heaven with him." This proverb means that one man's promotion to a higher, more influential position leads to the good fortune of his family and friends.

一日不见 如隔三秋

yí rì bú jiàn rú gé sān qiū

Missing you one day is
like being separated for three autumns

古时候有个小伙子，和一位美丽的姑娘相爱了。可是，那位姑娘却不能经常和他见面。她要帮助父母做很多事情：要去采苎（zhù）麻，用来织夏布；要去采香蒿，用来祭祀；要去采艾草，用来治病。小伙子度日如年，无时不在思念自己的心上人。于是他就写了一首诗，倾吐自己对恋人的相思之情：

彼采葛兮。一日不见，如三月兮！
彼采萧兮。一日不见，如三秋兮！
彼采艾兮。一日不见，如三岁兮！

这首诗，以夸张和比喻的方法，表达了对爱人的强烈思念，因而广为后世所传诵。后来"一日不见，如隔三秋"用以形容迫切的思念心情。

A long time ago, there was a young lad who fell in love with a beautiful young girl. Yet alas, this young girl could seldom meet with him, for she had to help her parents with many different chores, such as gathering ramie grass in preparation for knitting summer clothes, gathering artemisia grass for ancestral sacrifices, and gathering mugwort grass for medicinal purposes. To the young lad, every day felt like a year: day and night he could not stop thinking about his beloved. He therefore composed a poem expressing his deep-felt yearning for her:

> "Alas, she has gone to gather ramie grass. Each day I see her not is as the passing of three months.
> Alas, she has gone to gather artemisia grass. Each day I see her not is as the passing of three autumns.
> Alas, she has gone to gather mugwort grass. Each day I see her not is as the passing of three years."

This poem uses similes which exaggerate the powerful emotions a lover feels towards his beloved. This poem became widely circulated in later generations. In its present form, "missing you one day is like being separated for three autumns" is an analogy which expresses an overwhelming desire and yearning for someone or something.

人 之 将 死 其 言 也 善

rén zhī jiāng sǐ qí yán yě shàn

The words of a dying man are good words

孔子的弟子曾参病得快要死了，鲁国大夫仲孙捷去探望他。仲孙捷是个不拘小节的人，平时言谈举止随便而不庄重，所以曾参见他来了，就劝导他说："鸟快要死时，鸣声是悲哀的；人快要死时，说出话来是善意的。我现在是快要死的人，想请你今后在待人接物上注意三方面：第一，容貌要严肃，这样可以避免别人对你无礼和不敬；第二，脸色要端庄，这样容易取得别人的信任；第三，说话时要推敲言辞和声调，这样可以避免粗野和错误。"仲孙捷听了，深受感动，连连点头称是。

后来，人们用"人之将死，其言也善"说明人在快死的时候，所说的话常是善意而又于人有益的。

While Zeng Shen, a student of Confucius, was dying on his sickbed, Zhong Sunjie, a doctor from the State of Lu, paid him a visit. Zhong Sunjie was a man unconcerned with trivial matters. He generally did not take himself too seriously, informal in manner and in speech. Therefore, when Zeng Shen met him on his deathbed, he gave him the following advice: "This old bird is about to die and his last chirp is full of sorrow. When a man is about to die, he will speak good-intentioned words. I am now about to die, and would like to leave you with three pieces of advice regarding your treatment of people: First, carry a serious face in public lest others treat you impolitely and disrespectfully; secondly, look dignified so that others may find it easy to put their trust in you; and thirdly, when you speak, weigh your words carefully and use a careful tone of voice in order to avoid boorishness and mistakes." Zhong Sunjie was deeply moved by the dying man's advice, continuously nodding his head in agreement with every word.

Later the proverb "the words of a dying man are good words" came to mean that the advice given by a man on his deathbed are often words of good intention which will benefit the receiver.

人生七十古来稀

rén shēng qī shí gǔ lái xī

It is rare for a man to live to 70

唐代"安史之乱"平定以后,唐肃宗率领朝臣回到收复了的京城长安。当时诗人杜甫在朝中担任左拾遗官职。左拾遗是个八品官,奉禄低微,很难供养全家,因此日子过得比较艰难。 生平喜欢饮酒的杜甫,常常在朝中遇到不平之事,再加上自身受到弄权奸臣的排挤,心情不好,因而更要饮酒解闷。没有钱,他就去典卖衣物,换钱买酒。

　　有一天,他喝了几杯酒后,一时心情激愤,挥笔写了两首七言律诗,题为《曲江二首》。 其中一首的前四句这样写道:

　　朝回日日典春衣,每日江头尽醉归。

　　酒债寻常随处有,人生七十古来稀。

　　这几句诗写出杜甫的穷困潦倒和他苦闷的心情。其中"人生七十古来稀"一句,是古代流传下来的一条谚语,说明人活到七十岁是很难得的。

In the Tang Dynasty (618–907), after a rebellion raised by general An Lushan and Shi Siming was put down in 763, Emperor Suzong led his courtiers back to the recovered capital of Changan. At the time, Du Fu, a poet, was serving as a low-ranking official. Because of his low-salaried position, he had great difficulty supporting his family and lived a very hard life. Du Fu faced many injustices during his court career, with many power-hungry, unscrupulous officials trying to squeeze him out of his position. Depressed, he, a lover of wine, sought even more to drown his sorrows by drinking. In his penniless condition, he would pawn his clothes and use the money he got back to buy more wine.

One day, after a few drinks, he suddenly became particularly inspired. He picked up his brush and penned two seven-character poems entitled *Two Poems Written at the Qujiang River*. One of the poems begins with the following lines:

Returning from court daily, I pawn off my summer clothes.
Daily I drink at the banks of Qujiang, 'til drunken homeward I go.
Wine debts my companion where'ere I go, for a man to live to 70, how rare indeed!

This short poem succinctly captures the poverty-stricken and frustrated existence of Du Fu as well as his general mood of depression. The proverb "it is rare for a man to live to 70" passed down from ancient times to the present, expresses that it is indeed a rare occurrence for a man to live to the age of 70.

八 仙 过 海　 各 显 神 通

bā　xiān　guò　hǎi　　gè　xiǎn　shén　tōng

**When the Eight Immotals cross the sea,
each shows his or her own ability**

传说古时候有八位神仙，个个神通广大，法力无边。他们的名字是：铁拐李、韩湘子、吕洞宾，蓝采和、汉钟离、张果老、曹国舅、何仙姑。有一次，天宫的王母娘娘在瑶池举办蟠桃盛会，邀请他们去参加，八仙结伴前往，驾起祥云，朝天宫而去。当众仙来到东海岸边时，只见浩瀚大海一望无际，波涛滚滚，奔腾呼啸。吕洞宾笑着对大家说："我们每人用自己的宝物过海，怎么样？"大家齐声叫好。

　　铁拐李先掷铁拐于涛谷之中，仙杖立刻变成一只龙舟。他轻身一跃，坐了上去。汉钟离投鼓于水，盘腿而坐；鼓随浪涡旋转，悠然自得。张果老倒骑在驴背上，扬鞭催驴，甚是得意。吕洞宾站在箫管上，劈波斩浪，威风凛凛。韩湘子投下花篮，顿时香气袭人，龙宫宫女蜂拥而至，采篮中鲜花，并挥动长袖，抬他过海。蓝采和投下拍板（一种由三块板组成的打击乐器），化作一叶扁舟，飘然而行。何仙姑、曹国舅也不甘示弱，分别抛出玉版和竹罩，似乘舻舳，轻快如飞。八仙于万顷碧波中各自显示了超凡的本领，不大一会，渡过了东海。

　　根据这个故事，后人概括出"八仙过海，各显神通"这一谚语，用以比喻人们各自施展自己的本领去完成相同的任务。

Legend has it that in ancient times there were the Eight Immortals, each possessing special abilities and supernatural powers. Their names were Iron Cane Li, Han Xiangzi, Lü Dongbin, Lan Caihe, Han Zhongli, Zhang Guolao, Cao Guojiu, and He Xiangu. One day, the Queen Mother of the Heavenly Palace invited them to the Peach Festival held at the Garden of the Immortals. So, riding on an auspicious cloud, together the Eight Immortals headed out towards the Heavenly Palace. As they neared the edge of the Eastern Sea, they were greeted by a vast ocean, which extended as far as the eye could see, and was teeming with raging waves. Lü Dongbin turned to his companions and chuckled, "How about crossing this sea with each one's precious object?" The suggestion met with a quick response from the rest of them.

Iron Cane Li took the lead by casting his iron cane into the heart of the wave trough. Immediately, the cane turned into a dragon boat which Li hopped upon and took across. Han Zhongli followed suit by casting his drum into the ocean and then sitting cross-legged on it. His drum was quickly caught up in the swirling of the waves and carried him leisurely to the other side. Zhang Guolao proudly sat backwards on the back of his donkey and whipped his donkey on to the other side. Lü Dongbin stood on his *xiao*, or vertical bamboo flute, and haughtily cut a swath through the waves. Han Xiangzi threw in a basket of flowers and soon the air was filled with the aroma of the flowers. The maidens of the Dragon Palace swarmed up from the bottom of the sea to gather up the fresh flowers. Then, with a wave of their long flowing sleeves, carried him across the ocean. Lan Caihe tossed a board in the sea, which carried him across the water like a small boat. He Xiangu and Cao Guojiu, not wanting to be outdone, respectively flung in a jade board and a bamboo shade which briskly conveyed them to the other side. In the face of this boundless expanse of blue water, the Eight Immortals

15

demonstrated their supernatural powers one after another. Soon they landed safely on the other side of the Eastern Sea.

This legend gave rise to the proverb "when the Eight Immortals cross the sea, each shows his or her own ability," which means different individuals can accomplish the same task in different ways.

士 为 知 己 者 死

shì   wèi   zhī   jǐ   zhě   sǐ

A gentleman will die for his confidant

春秋时期，晋国有位侠士名叫豫让。他先后投奔大贵族范氏和中行氏，可这两人都不重用他，只把他当作一般的食客看待。于是豫让离开他们，来到另一个贵族智伯那里。智伯很尊敬、宠信豫让，以上宾的礼遇对待他。这使豫让非常感激，暗暗下决心报答智伯。后来晋国贵族赵襄子联合韩、魏两国打败智伯，并杀死了他。智伯的亲信党羽四下逃散，豫让也逃到深山里躲避。

　　豫让在深山中过了几个月，感到风声不那么紧了，就打算出山替智伯报仇。他自言自语地说："士为知己者死，女为悦己者容。智伯了解我，信任我，我一定替他报仇而死！"于是，豫让改名换姓，装扮成一个泥瓦匠来到赵襄子宫中，为赵襄子粉刷厕所墙壁。他怀中揣着一把匕首，准备伺机刺杀赵襄子。结果事情败露，豫让被抓了起来。赵襄子念他忠于主子，是个义士，放走了他。后来豫让再次行刺，又被赵襄子抓住，被杀掉了。

　　后来，人们用"士为知己者死"比喻大丈夫甘愿为知己献出生命，也比喻人才甘为知人善任者效力。

During the Spring and Autumn Period (770–476 B.C.), there was a knight from the State of Jin named Yu Rang. He successively sought refuge at the households of noblemen Fan and Zhongxing, but neither man appreciated his importance, instead they treated him like just another mouth to feed. For this reason, Yu Rang left them and went to seek lodging at the home of another nobleman named Zhi Bo. Zhi Bo highly esteemed Yu Rang and treated him as an honored guest. To show his gratitude, Yu Rang secretly determined in his heart to one day repay Zhi Bo's kindness. Later, Zhao Xiangzi, an aristocrat from the State of Jin, joined forces with the states of Han and Wei and defeated Zhi Bo and his men, killing him in the takeover. Many of Zhi Bo's trusted followers fled helter-skelter, and Yu Rang, too, went into hiding in the deep mountains.

Having hidden in the mountains for a few months, Yu Rang felt that the situation had now calmed down a little and decided to come out of hiding to avenge the death of Zhi Bo. He said to himself, "A gentleman will die for his confidant just as a woman will doll herself up for her admirer. Zhi Bo understood me and trusted me; I must avenge his death even if it means giving up my own life!" Changing his name and, disguising himself as a bricklayer, he gained entry into the court of Zhao Xiangzi ostensibly to whitewash the bathroom walls. Hiding a dagger in his clothes, he waited for the opportune moment to assassinate Zhao Xiangzi. But before he had a chance, Zhao Xiangzi discovered his plot and had him captured. Regarding Yu Rang as a just man and a man faithful to his master, Zhao let him go. Later, when Yu Rang was caught in his second assassination attempt, Zhao had him executed.

Later the saying "a gentleman will die for his confidant" became a proverb. In ancient times, it meant that a real man would be willing to sacrifice his life for his confidant. Now it has come to mean that a man of talent is more than willing to do his best for a superior who trusts in his abilities.

士 别 三 日 当 刮 目 相 看
shì bié sān rì dāng guā mù xiāng kàn

After three days,
view a gentleman with new eyes

三国时期，吴侯孙权手下有一位年轻的将领名叫吕蒙。他作战勇敢，胆量过人，跟随孙权驰骋疆场，屡建功勋，因此深为孙权器重。但由于他自幼家境贫寒，没有读过多少书，孙权有心提拔他担任更重要的职务，又怕他难以胜任。于是就把他找来，劝他多读些书，以增长知识，充实自己。孙权说："你天资聪颖，年龄并不算太大，如能勤奋学习，一定长进很快。过去汉光武帝刘秀领兵作战时，手不释卷，曹操也自称老而好学。你为什么不能以他们为榜样，勉励自己学习呢？"

吕蒙听了这番话，深受感动。从那以后，除了行军打仗，他把时间都用来苦读苦学。没过几年，读的书竟超过了一般的儒生。

一次，吴军新任都督鲁肃来到吕蒙的驻防营地。经过交谈，发现他引经据典，谈古论今。鲁肃又惊又喜，站起身来拍着吕蒙的肩膀说："我一直以为你能武不能文，没想到你的学识如此渊博，已经完全不是当年的吕蒙了！"吕蒙听了也有些得意，笑着说："士别三日，当刮目相看，何况我们分别了很长时间呢！"

这条谚语告诉人们人是可以改变的，因而不能总用老眼光看待别人。

During the Three Kingdoms Period (220–280), there was a young general named Lü Meng who served under Sun Quan, founder of the Kingdom of Wu. He had fought in many battles under Sun's command, and was known for his extraordinary valor. Because of his repeated military exploits, he was highly esteemed by Sun Quan. But Lü Meng's one shortcoming was his lack of a strong educational background, for, in his childhood, he had been raised in a poor family.

Sun Quan wanted to promote him to more prominent posts of power, but was worried about his lack of qualifications. Sun Quan therefore sent for Lü Meng and advised him to spend more time reading books and expanding his knowledge in order to better prepare himself for the future. Sun Quan exhorted him, "You are naturally very bright and are still young. If you apply yourself diligently to your studies, I am sure you will improve quickly. In the past, when Liu Xiu, Emperor Guang Wu of the Han Dynasty, led his army to war, he always had a book in his hand. Even Cao Cao described himself as old but always an avid learner of new things. Why can't you follow their examples to encourage yourself to study harder?"

Lü Meng was deeply moved by these words. From then on, in between marches and battles he spent his time studying hard. In just a few years, he had read more books than the average Confucian scholar.

One time, the new commander-in-chief of the Kingdom of Wu, Lu Su, met Lü Meng at his camp. In their conversation, the commander-in-chief was pleasantly surprised by the man's amazing ability to quote the classics while talking past and present. Lu Su stood up and, patting Lü Meng on the shoulder, said, "I always thought you were just a man of war. Who would have imagined that you were a man of such erudition — you are not the same Lü Meng as I remembered!" Lü Meng proudly replied with a chuckle, "When you have been separated from a gentleman for three days, you should use new eyes to view him, not to mention the fact that we haven't seen each other for a long time!"

This proverb means that a person can change so we should not judge him by old standards.

大 意 失 荆 州

dà   yì   shī   jīng   zhōu

Because of negligence, Jingzhou is lost

刘备建立蜀国后,其军事重镇荆州(今湖北江陵)一直由关羽把守。

一天,东吴的谋士诸葛谨来到荆州,替孙权的儿子向关羽求亲,不料关羽勃然大怒,说:"我虎女怎能嫁给他犬子!"诸葛谨回去后如实讲了。孙权十分恼火,决心夺取荆州,以泄心中之愤。大将吕蒙说:"关羽所忧虑的是我。我想装病辞职,这样关羽就不会再提防东吴;然后乘其不备偷袭他,即可成功。"孙权听从了这个主意,就派一位无名小将去接替吕蒙的职位。

关羽听到吕蒙因病辞职的消息,十分高兴,不再担心东吴军队会对荆州有所威胁,于是就把大部分荆州人马调去攻打曹操军队占领的樊城(今湖北襄樊)。部下王甫提醒他要提防东吴偷袭,他就让王甫在沿江建造了一些烽火台,如果东吴军队渡江侵犯,就让士兵夜里放火,白天放炮。他看到烟火后立即带兵来营救。

吕蒙探听到关羽已率兵离开荆州,便选择了一批勇敢而机灵的士兵,扮成商人,驾驶十余只快船,日夜兼程,直奔荆州。当经过烽火台被守卒盘问时,吴国兵都说:"我们是商人。"同时,将金钱财物送给守烽火台的官员,因而所有船只都被允许停靠岸边。到了半夜,吴国士兵一齐杀出,把烽火台上的官军全部捉住,然后威逼他们带路去荆州城下叫门。荆州守军见是自己人，果真开了城门。吕蒙率领东吴士兵一拥而入，不折一兵一卒便夺取了荆州。

根据这个故事，人们概括出"大意失荆州"这个谚语，用以比喻由于疏忽大意造成了重大损失。

Since the Kingdom of Shu was established in Sichuan, Jingzhou (present-day Jiangling County in Hubei Province), which was far away from the capital of Shu, had been guarded by General Guan Yu.

One day, Zhuge Jin, a military advisor of the Kingdom of Wu, arrived at Jingzhou and made a marriage proposal to Guan Yu's daughter on behalf of Sun Quan's son. To his surprise, Guan Yu flew into a temper and retorted, "How could I ever let my daughter marry that dog!" Zhuge Jin went back and reported exactly what he had been told. A furious Sun Quan determined to capture Jingzhou in order to vent his anger. Major General Lü Meng advised him, "I am the one Guan Yu is concerned about. Let me pretend to be ill and resign from my post. This way Guan Yu will let down his guard against us. Then, when the time is ripe, we can attack him by taking him unawares and take over Jingzhou." Sun Quan took his advice and replaced Lü Meng with an unknown general.

When Guan Yu heard about Lü Meng's sick leave, he became overjoyed and no longer worried about the threat of an attack on Jingzhou from the Wu armies. He consequently dispatched the majority of his Jingzhou men to attack Cao Cao's troops at Fancheng (present-day Xiangfan County in Hubei Province). One of his subordinates, Wang Pu, warned him about the possibility of Wu's attack. So he let Wang Pu build a few beacon-fire towers along the riverbank. If the Wu troops crossed the river and encroached upon their territory, Wang Pu was to let his soldiers set fires by night and use smoke signals by day. Once Guan Yu saw the fire or smoke, he would come to their rescue.

When Lü Meng heard that Guan Yu had left Jingzhou with his troops, he hand-picked a group of brave and clever soldiers who dressed up as merchants, embarked on a dozen or so boats, and traveled day and night until they reached Jingzhou. When they were questioned at a beacon tower, they answered, "We are merchants." They then gave money and gifts to the guards, who then allowed them to dock their boats in the harbor. In the middle of the night, the Wu soldiers launched a surprise attack, capturing all the officers and soldiers guarding the beacon tower. The captives were then coerced to lead the way to the gate of Jingzhou and ask for entry. When the guards saw that it was their own men asking for entry and opened the gate, Lü Meng and his men swept into the city, and captured Jingzhou without losing a single soldier.

This story was later summarized into the proverb "because of negligence, Jingzhou is lost," a metaphorical expression referring to the suffering of a great loss due to negligence and carelessness.

万 事 俱 备 只 欠 东 风

wàn shì jù bèii zhǐ qiàn dōng fēng

Everything is ready,
and all that we need is an east wind

公元 208 年，曹操亲自率领八十万大军，企图一举消灭刘备和孙权。危急关头，诸葛亮出使东吴，说服了孙权，两家联合，共同对付曹操。孙权任命周瑜为"大都督"统率三军人马，迎战曹操。

周瑜与诸葛亮经周密研究决定采用"火攻"。周瑜先用"苦肉计"，寻错把老将黄盖痛打一顿，然后让黄盖暗中派人送信给曹操，说自己不堪忍受屈辱，一有时机，就驾驶粮船，前来投降。同时，谋士庞统也去诈降，并向曹操献上"连环计"。他说只要把大小船只的首尾用铁环扣住，连成一体，船就不会再晃动，不习水战的北方将士也就不会晕船了。曹操不知是计，竟信以为真照办了。

一切准备停当。这天，周瑜站在江边，观望对岸曹营动静。忽然迎面刮来一阵西北风，周瑜不禁心头一惊，猛然想起此时正值隆冬，天天刮着西北风，而火攻必须借助东风才能成功。这可怎么办呢？周瑜大叫一声，倒在地上，口吐鲜血。

诸葛亮得知周瑜病了，前往探视。他对周瑜说："我有一方，包治你病。"说罢提笔写了十六个字：欲破曹公，宜用火攻；万事俱备，只欠东风。周瑜看了便笑着说："先生已知我的病根，将如何治疗？"诸葛亮懂得天文气象，他根据某些物象的反映和变化，推断出风向将转为东风，便说："我曾学过呼风唤雨，让我借三日东风与你。"周瑜一听这话，病顿时好了七八分。

诸葛亮让人筑起法坛，祭天借风。三更时分，果然刮起东南风。周瑜立即让黄盖去诈降，二十只装有芦苇、干柴、鱼油的大船，趁着东风，箭一般驶向曹军水寨。最初，曹操还以为黄盖驾着粮船来降，等这些船只接近曹营突然起火时，才知上当，但是为时已晚。孙刘联军乘机进攻，结果，连在一起的曹军战船被大火烧得精光，曹操本人也差一点送了性命。

"万事俱备，只欠东风"这一谚语比喻做一件事，其他条件都已具备，只缺最重要的条件。

In the year of 208, Cao Cao, who was posthumously named Emperor Wu Di of the Kingdom of Wei, personally led an army of 800,000 in an attempt to defeat the troops of Liu Bei and Sun Quan in a single strike. At this critical juncture, Zhuge Liang embarked on a diplomatic mission to persuade Sun Quan to unite with Liu Bei in fending off Cao Cao. Sun Quan appointed Zhou Yu as commander-in-chief of his army to prepare the struggle against Cao Cao. Zhou Yu and Zhuge Liang devised the special strategy of "attacking with fire." Using the ruse of inflicting injury upon oneself to gain the enemy's confidence, Zhou Yu gave old general Huang Gai a sound beating. Huang then had a secret letter delivered to Cao Cao, saying that he had had his fill of humiliation at the hand of Zhou and, at the first opportunity, he would take a grain boat and turn himself over. Under Zhou's direction, military advisor Pang Tong also feigned surrender and offered Cao Cao the "shrewd plan for connecting the boats." Pang said that if all the boats were linked stem to stern in a line with iron rings, the boats would no longer rock, and the northern troops, unaccustomed to fighting on the river, would no longer get sick. Cao, failing to see through the trick, accepted the advice.

Now everything was ready for the attack on Cao Cao. One day, Zhou Yu stood on the riverbank, spying on the movements in Cao Cao's camp on the other side. All of a sudden, there arose a northwesterly wind. An uncontrollable fear caught him as he realized the northwesterly winds could become his undoing, for the success of the "fire attack" hinged on the help of an easterly wind. What could be done? With a loud cry he fell over, blood foaming up in his mouth.

When Zhuge Liang heard that Zhou Yu was sick, he went to see him. Zhuge Liang said, "I have a prescription which is sure to cure you." He wrote the following words for Zhou Yu:

To break Cao's back

with fire we attack.
Everything is set, save
the east wind we lack!*

Zhou Yu read these words and responded with a chuckle, "Sir, since you already know the root of my sickness, how do you propose to cure it?" Zhuge Liang had some knowledge about astronomy. According to the way the weather responded to certain natural phenomenon, he deduced that the wind would soon be turning east. He explained to Zhou Yu: "In the past, I have learned how to summon the wind and invoke the rain. Now let me borrow three days of east wind to assist you." Hearing these words, Zhou Yu immediately felt better.

Zhuge Liang then had an altar built to offer sacrifices to Heaven in order to borrow the wind. At the third watch of the night, a southeasterly wind did arise as predicted. Zhou Yu immediately sent Huang Gai to feign surrender to Cao Cao. Carried by the easterly wind, twenty large boats stocked full with reed, fagots, and fish oil swiftly made their way towards Cao Cao's naval camp. At first Cao Cao believed that Huang Gai was giving himself up along with the grain boats. Only when the boats drew near to Cao's camp and a fire suddenly broke out on the boats did he know he had been deceived. But it was already too late. The armies of Sun and Liu quickly seized the opportunity to launch an attack. Eventually, Cao Cao's warships, chained together with iron rings, were completely consumed in the conflagration. Cao Cao himself scarcely escaped with his life.

The proverb "everything is ready, and all that we need is an east wind " means that all is ready in a certain situation except what is crucial.

---

* This is quoted from *The Three Kingdoms* translated by Moss Robert, Foreign Languages Press, Beijing.

32

才 说 曹 操　曹 操 就 到

cái shuō cáo cāo　cáo cāo jiù dào

Just after you mention Cao Cao,
he shows up

　　东汉末年，吕布领兵攻占本是曹操地盘的山东濮阳。曹操不肯罢休，又率兵来反攻。吕布的谋士陈宫向吕布献计，让濮阳城内一个姓田的巨富派人去曹营中对曹操说："吕布如今不在濮阳，城中空虚，希望曹将军夜间来攻城。只要看到城上插有白旗，上面写有"义"字，那就是暗号。"

　　曹操信以为真，当天晚上就领兵攻城。来到城下，果然看到城头插有"义"字白旗。不一会，城门被人打开，吊桥放落。曹操领兵策马而入，直到州衙，却不见一人。曹操知道中计，忙拨马回头，大叫"退兵"。可是为时已晚，只听一声炮响，喊杀声四起。曹操慌忙向北门冲去。一路上，他的人马被截杀死伤大半。正行间，火光之中，撞见吕布挺戟跃马而来。曹操赶忙用袖子把脸遮住，只听吕布问道："曹操在哪里？"曹操用手往前一指，说："前面那个骑黄马的就是曹操！"吕布丢下曹操，向前追去。

　　曹操见骗过吕布，赶紧拨马回头，向东门逃跑。这时曹操手下的大将典韦正在打听曹操下落，却正好曹操来到。典韦护卫着曹操杀出一条血路，终于逃出城去。

　　根据这个故事，后人概括出"才说曹操，曹操就到"这个谚语，用来形容正提到某个人，这个人恰好来到。

Towards the end of the Eastern Han Dynasty (25–220), Lü Bu led an expedition and captured Puyang City in Shandong Province, which belonged to Cao Cao. But Cao Cao refused to give up so easily, and led his troops in a counterattack. Lü Bu's advisor Chen Gong advised him to let an affluent man in Puyang, surnamed Tian, to send the following message to Cao Cao: "Lü Bu is not in Puyang now, and the city is empty. I hope General Cao will come to take back the city at nightfall. Once you see a white flag on the city wall bearing the word "Justice," that will be the secret signal for your entry into the city."

Cao Cao, took the message as true, and on that very night, led his troops to attack the city. As he neared the city wall, he saw the word "Justice" on the white flag on top of the city wall just as he was informed. After a while, the city gate was swung open and the drawbridge lowered. Cao Cao led his army into the city, whipping his horse onward. When they reached the prefecture's government office, they found it empty. Cao Cao then knew he had been tricked and hastily turned his horse around, shouting to his troops, "Retreat!" But it was too late. Before he knew it, he was surrounded by the roar of booming cannons and the murderous cries of the enemy. The panic-stricken Cao Cao quickly rushed for the North Gate, and most of his men and horses were killed or wounded in the process. As Cao Cao was battling his way out through the blaze, he saw Lü Bu holding an halberd erect in his hand and galloping towards him. Cao Cao hurriedly covered his face with his sleeves as he heard Lü Bu ask, "Where is Cao Cao?" Cao Cao pointed, saying, "That guy in front of you riding the yellow horse is Cao Cao." Lü Bu left Cao Cao and dashed forward and continued his chase.

Seeing that Lü Bu had fallen for his trick, Cao Cao hastily turned his horse around and rode towards the East Gate. Just then, one of Cao Cao's subordinates, General Dian Wei, was asking about the whereabouts of Cao Cao. It was at this very moment that Cao Cao showed up. Dian Wei then protected Cao Cao, fighting his way out of the city.

This story was later summarized into the proverb "just after you mention Cao Cao, he shows up." It is used when a person just happens to show up right after you talk about him.

千 丈 之 堤　溃 于 蚁 穴

qiān zhàng zhī　dī　kuì yú yǐ xué

A thousand-mile dyke can collapse
due to an ant-hole

36

韩非是战国时期的一位大文学家。有一次，他在一篇文章中论述防微杜渐的重要性时，这样说："千丈的河堤，会由于蝼蛄蚂蚁一类的小虫钻洞而溃决，百尺高的房屋，会因为烟囱缝隙里冒出的烟火而焚烧。过去白圭（战国时人，以善于治水闻名）兴修水利，总是经常巡视河堤，发现穴窟赶紧堵塞；有经验的老人总是经常检查烟囱。及时堵塞缝隙。所以白圭治水从未发生过水患。有经验的老人家里也从未发生过火灾。"

接着韩非讲了一个因忽视细节而酿成大祸的故事。

从前名医扁鹊去见蔡国国君蔡桓公。他仔细打量了好久说："君王身上有毛病，在表皮部位；如果不治，怕会越来越重。"蔡桓公说："瞎说，我哪有什么病？"过了十几天，扁鹊又来见蔡桓公说："君王的病已发展到肌肉里面，不治将会越来越严重。"蔡桓公听了，摇摇头不作声。又过了十几天，扁鹊再一次来见蔡桓公，恳切地说："君王的病已进入肠胃，再不治就不好治了。"蔡桓公听后很不高兴，不理睬扁鹊。再过了十几天，当扁鹊见到蔡桓公时，他一句话不说转身就走。桓公感到奇怪，便派人去问扁鹊。扁鹊对来人说："当病在表皮时，贴上块膏药就可以治好；在肌肉里时，可用针灸疗法排除毒气；在肠胃里时还可以服用汤药，驱赶病魔。但当病侵入骨髓深处，那可就无药可救了。现在桓公的病已侵入骨髓，我因此无话可说了。"

没多长时间，蔡桓公就病死了。

韩非讲完这个故事后说道："治病要趁其尚在表皮时去治。这是因为病情轻微时便于医治。任何灾祸都像疫病一样，有它的萌芽状态，聪明人总是懂得及早处理方可转危为安的道理。"

后来，人们用"千丈之堤，溃于蚁穴"比喻忽视小的漏洞，将会酿成大祸，因此要防微杜渐。

Han Fei was a literary master during the Warring States Period (475–221 B.C.). In an essay expounding the importance of nipping evil in the bud, he once wrote, "Even a thousand-mile river dyke can collapse because of the holes bored into it by such insects as crickets and ants, just as a hundred-foot-tall house can burn down because of the little smoke and fire that emanates from the cracks of a chimney. In the past, when Bai Gui, a specialist on water conservancy, started constructing a water conservancy project, he would often make inspection tours of the river dyke and lose no time in patching up any holes he discovered. Older people with more experience often check on their chimneys and immediately seal up any cracks they see. Therefore while Bai Gui was in charge of the water conservancy project, there never was a flood problem, just as older people with more experience never encounter the danger of a fire starting from their chimneys."

Han Fei then proceeded to tell the story of a man whose neglect of a little detail cost him his life.

There once was a famous doctor named Bian Que who went to see Duke Huan of the State of Cai. After a detailed and lengthy physical examination of the duke, he said, "You have a skin disease on your body. If you don't take care of it, I'm afraid it will get worse." Duke Huan replied, "Nonsense! I am perfectly healthy!" A fortnight later, Bian Que came to see the duke again and told him, "Your Highness' sickness has now spread into your muscles. If you don't get it cured now, it will grow even more serious." Duke Huan shook his head, and said nothing. Another fortnight later, Bian Que came once more and told the duke earnestly, "Your Highness, your sickness has now entered into your stomach and intestinal area; if you don't heal it now, it will be very difficult to heal in the future." Duke Huan was very displeased after hearing this, yet continued to ignore Bian Que's words. Three fortnights later, Bian Que visited again, but on appraisal of the situation he turned around and left without speaking a single word. Duke Huan felt it very strange and sent someone to make an inquiry of the doctor. This is what Bian Que told him: "When the duke's sickness was just a mere skin irritation, using a medicine patch would have cured it; when it became a muscle disease, acupuncture could have rooted out the poison; even when it became a stomach problem, he could have taken some decoction to usher out the virus. But now the sickness has penetrated deeply into his bone marrow, there is nothing more for me to say." Not long after, the duke died.

After relating this story, Han Fei explained, "When curing an illness, it is best to cure it while it is still skin deep. That is because a small sickness is easy to cure. Every disaster is just like a severe illness; it also has a budding process. Therefore the wise man knows to deal with the problem in its earliest stages, turning a potentially dangerous situation into a safe one.

The proverb "a thousand-mile dyke can collapse due to an ant-hole" is now used to mean that the neglect or overlooking of a little loophole can bring disaster. That is why people are requested to nip evil and trouble in the bud.

千里送鹅毛礼轻情义重

qiān lǐ sòng é máo lǐ qīng qíng yì zhòng

A goose feather sent from thousands of miles away is a present little in size but rich in meaning

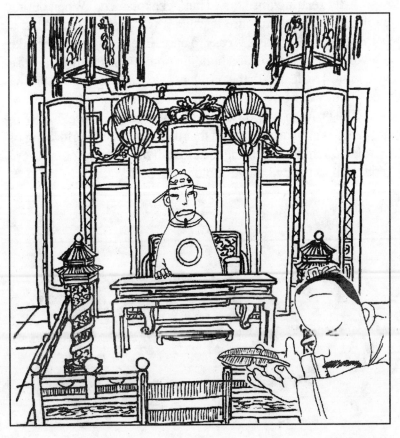

唐朝时，有个地方官得到一只名贵的天鹅。他想讨好皇帝，便派一名叫缅伯高的人带着天鹅去京城进贡。当时正是六月天，天气炎热，气温很高，一路上缅伯高小心翼翼，生怕出事。这天路过沔（miǎn）阳湖，缅伯高怕热坏了天鹅，就把它从笼子里拿出来，想在湖边给天鹅洗洗澡。不料，天鹅猛的一挣，竟飞跑了。慌忙之中，缅伯高只抓到一片鹅毛。没有办法，他只好拿着这片鹅毛去见皇帝。到朝廷之上，他双手捧着鹅毛，把情由述说一遍，末了又口吟一首诗：

将鹅贡唐朝，山高路远遥。
沔阳湖失去，倒地哭号号。
上复唐天子，可饶缅伯高。
礼轻情意重，千里送鹅毛。

皇帝见他言词恳切，便留下鹅毛，让他回去了。
此谚语用以说明礼物虽然微薄，情意却很深厚。

During the Tang Dynasty, there was a local official who received a rare and precious swan. In order to please the emperor, he sent a man named Mian Bogao to take the swan to the capital as a gift to the emperor. It was the sixth lunar month, and the weather was very hot. The whole way, Mian took special care to make sure nothing would go wrong. One day, he reached the Mianyang Lake. Afraid that the goose would die of the heat, he took the goose out of its cage and wanted to give it a little bath by the lakeside. But to his surprise, the swan suddenly burst out of his grip and flew away. In a flurry, all Mian Bogao got on his hands was just a single swan feather. He had no choice but to bring this feather to the emperor. When he arrived at the court, with both hands he presented the feather to the emperor and explained what had happened. He concluded with the recitation of the following poem:

> I meant to bring a swan to pay tribute to the Tang court,
> Despite the long journey punctuated by towering mountains.
> When I lost the swan by the Mianyang Lake, I fell to the
>   ground and cried in helplessness.
> Now that I've reported to you, the Son of Heaven of Tang.
>   Please show thy mercy upon Mian Bogao.
> Small as my gift is, rich it is with meaning.
> From thousands of miles afar I've brought you this swan
>   feather.

The emperor, impressed with his earnestness, received the feather, and let him return home.

This proverb is used to describe a gift that is little in size but full of meaning.

千 钱 买 邻　八 百 买 舍

qiān qián mǎi lín　bā bǎi mǎi shè

A thousand gold pieces buy a neighbor,
800 buy a home

南北朝时，梁朝朝廷中有一位大臣名叫吕僧珍。此人能征善战，足智多谋，在帮助梁高祖建立梁朝的过程中立下了赫赫功绩，深受皇帝的信任。但是吕僧珍从不居功自傲，为人处事，谦恭谨慎，清正廉洁，因而朝廷官员都很敬慕他，以能与他结交为荣。

当时，有个名叫宋季雅的人，为了能与吕僧珍做邻居，专门花高价购买吕僧珍住宅旁边的宅院。吕僧珍问他花了多少钱，他说："一千一百万。"吕僧珍不明白他为什么花这么大的价钱买一套住宅。宋季雅回答说："不贵，不贵，我是一百万买宅，一千万买邻。"

这个故事引申出"千钱买邻，八百买舍"的谚语，用以说明好的邻居比好的房舍重要得多。

During the Northern and Southern Dynasties (420–589), there was a famous minister named Lü Sengzhen in the Liang Dynasty. He was adept at warfare, wise and full of stratagems. Because he performed impressive military feats in helping Emperor Gao Zu establish the Liang Dynasty, the emperor had complete confidence in him. But Lü never claimed credit for himself or allowed himself to become arrogant, and he treated people and handed situations with modesty, courtesy, discretion and honesty. For this reason, he won the respect and admiration of many courtiers, who sought the honor of making his acquaintance.

At that time, there was a man named Song Jiya. In order to be a neighbor with Lü Sengzhen, he went out of his way and spent a fortune to procure a mansion next to Lü's house. When Lü Sengzhen asked him how much he spent on the mansion, he replied, "Eleven million pieces of gold." Lü wondered why he should have spent such an exorbitant amount for the house. To which Song Jiya replied, "That's not expensive at all, no, not at all. For I spent one million to buy the mansion, and 10 million to buy a neighbor like you."

This story later evolved into the proverb "a thousand gold pieces buy a neighbor, 800 buy a house," meaning it is much more important to have a good neighbor than a good house.

小时了了　大未必佳

xiǎo shí liǎo liǎo　dà wèi bì jiā

**If you are bright when you are young,
you may not necessarily amount to something
when you grow up**

东汉文学家孔融十岁的时候，随父亲到了洛阳。当时担任司隶校尉的李元礼颇有名望，要想见他很不容易，只有当时的名人雅士，或者李元礼的亲戚，门人才给通报。

一天，孔融来到李元礼的门前对守门人说："我是李家的亲戚。"经通报后，孔融被请到客厅就座，李元礼见到是个小孩，十分惊讶，就问："你和我有什么亲戚关系呢？"孔融回答："从前我的祖先孔子曾经拜您的祖先李伯阳（老子）为师，以此说来，我们是世交呀。"李元礼和在座的宾客听了，无不拍手称妙。此时一位名叫陈韪的人走了进来，别人就把孔融的话告诉了他。他不以为然地说："小时了了，大来必佳。"孔融马上反驳道："想来您小时候，必定是一个聪明的人。"陈韪听了，脸上红一阵，白一阵，半天讲不出话来。

这条谚语说明幼年聪明的人，长大以后不一定有出息。

When the famous Eastern Han Dynasty writer Kong Rong was ten years old, he went to Luoyang with his father. At the time, Li Yuanli was a man of renown and difficult to meet. Only when a distinguished scholar or his relative came to visit did his doorman care to let him know.

One day, Kong Rong arrived at Li Yuanli's house and told the doorman, "I am a relative of Li Yuanli." After his message was delivered to Li, Kong Rong was invited into the living room. When Li Yuanli saw that it was a child who was seated there, he asked in a surprised voice, "What blood relations do I have with you?" Kong Rong replied, "My ancestor Confucius was once a student of your ancestor Li Boyang (Lao Zi). That makes us at least old family friends, right?" After Li and the other guests who were present heard the boy's reply, they applauded. At the moment, a man named Chen Wei stepped into the room. After he was told of Kong Rong's answer, he was not impressed, and he said, "If a boy is clever when he is young, when he is older he may not necessarily amount to something." Kong Rong immediately rebutted, "Then I presume that you must be quite bright when you were young." Chen Wei's face turned pale, and for a long time he did not know what to say.

This proverb means that a person who is bright at an early age may not have a promising future when he grows up.

天 高 皇 帝 远

tiān gāo huáng dì yuǎn

Heaven is high and
the emperor is faraway

元朝末年，封建贵族过着穷奢极欲的生活。由于他们大肆挥霍国库银两，国家财政终于入不敷出。元朝政府便将危机转嫁给劳动人民，巧立名目，增加赋税。民众交纳不起，就抓进官府痛打。当时"卖官"之风盛行，用钱买得官爵的富豪，转过来利用权力拚命地掠夺侵吞国家资财，残害人民。人民走投无路，不得不举起义旗，进行反抗。当时在浙江东部农民起义队伍中流传着这样一首民谣：

天高皇帝远，民少相公多，*

一日三遍打，不反待如何！

后来，人们用"天高皇帝远"，说明离中央或主管部门远，不受约束。

*民少相公多："相公"是封建时代对官员的称呼。此句为夸张的说法，讥讽"卖官"之滥之多。

During the late Yuan Dynasty (1271–1368), the aristocrats lived in debauchery and dissipation. As they squandered large amounts of public funds, the royal treasury was pushed to the point of being unable to make ends meet. Shifting the crisis onto the laboring people, the government concocted various pretexts to levy heavier taxes. Those who could not pay up were arrested and beaten up. Bribes to "purchase official positions" were commonplace. The rich and the powerful who bought their way into official positions were given to appropriating property and victimizing the people. In desperation the people had no choice but to rise in rebellion. At the time the following folk rhyme was circulating among peasant rebels in east Zhejiang Province:

Heaven is high and the emperor is faraway, the people are few, yet officials abound.
Thrice each day we are beaten! We've got to rebel — it's now or never!

Later the proverb "heaven is high and the emperor is faraway" is used to describe the condition of unrestrained freedom enjoyed by those far away from the central authority and government control.

无 功 不 受 禄

wú gōng bù shòu lù

One should not receive a reward
for doing nothing

春秋时，有一次孔子带着他的弟子来到齐国，向齐景公宣传自己的政治主张。孔子是名人，齐景公虽然对他的政治主张不感兴趣，但还是很热情地接待他，并想把他网罗在自己手下。齐景公对孔子说："先生能到齐国来，我感到很荣幸，希望您能长期住下，帮助我治理国家。我想把廪(lǐn)丘(今山东郭城西)这块地方送给您作为封地，好吗？"孔子坚决推辞，没有接受，并当即向齐景公辞行。孔子走出门外，对他的弟子说："吾闻君子当功以受禄。今天我劝说景公推行'仁义'之道，景公还没有推行就赐给我廪丘。他这样做是太不了解我这个人了！"说罢，命令弟子赶紧驾车，离开齐国。

后来孔子的话演变为"无功不受禄"这个谚语，用以说明不能无故接受别人的恩惠。

During the Spring and Autumn Period, Confucius and his disciples once visited the State of Qi in order to propagate his political viewpoints to Duke Jing of Qi. Though the duke was uninterested in Confucius' political views, he nevertheless accorded him a warm welcome because of his good name. Furthermore, he hoped to enlist his services. The duke told Confucius, "Sir, I am honored that you could come and visit the State of Qi and hope that you would consider settling down here to help me govern my country. I would also like to enfeoff you with the land of Linqiu (west of present-day Yuncheng in Shandong Province), if you are willing to stay." Confucius declined his offer without hesitation, and quickly said his good-bye to the duke. As Confucius stepped out of the door, he turned to his disciples and said, "I have heard that a gentleman will only accept an emolument after he has done some work to deserve it. Today I advised the duke to carry out the way of benevolence and righteousness, yet before he has even begun implementing this policy, he offers me Linqiu. This shows that he really doesn't understand me!" After saying this, he immediately ordered his students to prepare his chariot and left the State of Qi.

Later this story evolved into the proverb "one should not receive a reward for doing nothing," which means one should not receive the kindness of another for no reason at all.

太公钓鱼　愿者上钩

tài gōng diào yú　yuàn zhě shàng gōu

Lord Jiang casts the line for
the fish which wants to be caught

商朝末年，有一个姓姜名尚字子牙的人，人称太公。太公本领出众，有匡世治国之才。他原在商纣王手下做大臣，因看不惯纣王为非作歹，残害百姓的暴行，弃官而逃，隐居在陕西渭水河畔。这地方是诸侯周文王姬昌的地盘。太公了解到文王胸怀大志，渴求人才，便每天坐在蟠溪河边钓鱼，等待着他的到来。

太公钓鱼与众不同，用的鱼钩是直的，也不挂鱼饵。钓鱼的时候，鱼钩高悬在水面三尺之上，同时他自言自语："鱼儿上钩来。"从他身边路过的渔民、樵夫常常取笑他，他也不在意，还随口作诗道："短杆长线守蟠溪，这个机关哪个知？只钓当朝君与相，何尝意在水中鱼！"太公就这样在蟠溪河畔度过了好多个年头。直到他八十岁那年，他的这种奇怪的钓鱼方法终于传到了文王耳内。文王想这个老翁如此古怪，其中必有缘故，于是派士兵去看个究竟。

太公见到士兵，睬也不睬，只顾钓鱼，口中喊着："钓，钓，钓！鱼儿不上钩，虾米瞎胡闹！"士兵回去把这情况告诉了文王，文王感到此人很不寻常，就又派朝中的大官去请太公。太公依旧不理睬，口中则喊着："钓，钓，钓！鱼儿不上钩，小鱼瞎胡闹！"大官一看这样，只好回去报告文王。文王心想此人定有超人的才能，于是就率领百官，抬着聘礼，亲自前往蟠溪邀请。太公这才随周文王入朝，做了丞相。从那以后，太公尽心尽力辅佐周文王治理国家。文王死后，他又辅佐周武王讨伐纣王，推翻了商朝，建立了周朝。

根据这个故事，后人概括出"太公钓鱼，愿者上钩"这个谚语，用以比喻做事出于自愿。

Towards the end of the Shang Dynasty (c. 16th-11th century B.C.), there was a man called Jiang Shang. His style name was Ziya, but everybody called him Lord Jiang. A man of extraordinary abilities, he was known especially for his superb administration of state affairs. He had served as a top official under King Zhou of Shang, but because he could not tolerate the wicked deeds of the king and his ruthless treatment of the people, he fled the court and became a recluse on the banks of Weishui River in Shaanxi Province. The place was the territory of Marquis King Wen of Zhou, known to Lord Jiang as an ambitious man who longed to recruit the best personnel available. So every day he would sit angling by a stream called Panxi River, waiting for King Wen to discover him.

The lord had a very peculiar angling style: he used a straight fish hook without any bait on it. As he kept his fish hook suspended three feet above the water, he would talk to himself: "C'mon fish, go for the hook." The fishermen and woodcutters passing by would often ridicule him, but he did not care, and even composed a poem which he muttered as he fished: "With short pole and long line I keep watch by Panxi River, yet who knows my true motive? I'm angling for kings and ministers, not for fish!"

And so Lord Jiang passed his time in this way on the bank of the river for a good many years. It was not until he reached the age of eighty that his strange angling method reached the ears of the king. Intrigued by this old man's eccentric ways, the king sent over a soldier to find out what was going on there.

When Lord Jiang saw the soldier coming, he paid no attention to him and kept on fishing. All the while he shouted, "To hook, to hook, to hook! The big fish hasn't gone for the hook, and yet here comes a little shrimp to mess around with me!" The soldier returned and reported what he had seen to the king. This convinced King Wen that he was quite an unusual man. So this time he sent over a high official to request Jiang's presence. Jiang again paid no attention to him and started to shout, "To hook, to hook, to hook! The big fish hasn't gone for the hook, and yet here comes a little fish to mess around with me!" When the official saw this situation, all he could do was to return and report what he saw to the king, who concluded that this man must be a man of exceptional abilities. He therefore gathered all his officials together and, carrying a special invitation gift, made a personal trip to Panxi River to greet him. It was in this manner that the king enlisted Lord Jiang as prime minister of Zhou. From that time onward, Lord Jiang dedicated all his effort to assisting King Wen in ruling the state. After the death of King Wen, he assisted King Wu of Zhou in a punitive expedition against King Zhou of Shang, which resulted in the overthrow of the Shang Dynasty and the establishment of the Zhou Dynasty.

This story later found expression in the proverb "lord Jiang casts the line for the fish which wants to be caught," a metaphor for doing something of one's own free will. It is also used to describe one who willingly falls into the snare.

五十步笑百步

wǔ shí bù xiào bǎi bù

Fifty steps laugh at 100 steps

战国时期，魏国自恃国力强盛，经常对其它诸侯国发动战争。有一天魏王对前来见他的孟子说："我对于国家真是费尽了心力。河内（今河南济源县一带）地方发生灾荒，我便把那里的灾民迁移一些到河东（今山西安泽县一带）去，同时还把河东的粮食调拨到河内救灾。遇到河东遭受饥荒的时候，我也是采取同样的办法。我曾经考察过邻国，没有哪一个国君能像我这样替老百姓着想的。可是邻国的百姓并没有因此而减少，我国的百姓也并不因此而增多，这是什么原因呢？"

孟子回答说："大王您喜欢战争，我就用战争作比喻。当战鼓敲响、刀枪相对的时候，有些胆小怕死的士兵竟抛下盔甲，扔下兵器向后逃跑。这些人中有的一口气跑了一百步停住脚，有的一口气跑了五十步停住脚。那些跑了五十步的士兵就耻笑跑了一百步的，说他们胆子太小。您说这样对吗？"

魏王说："当然不对。逃跑五十步也是逃跑，只不过没跑到一百步罢了。"

孟子说："大王如果明白这个道理，就不要再埋怨魏国的百姓不增多了。您虽然做了一些救灾的事，但并没有从根本上解决老百姓的温饱问题。您常常在农民耕种、收获的季节，去征兵、拉差，使农时违误，农田荒芜；富豪人家侵犯百姓，您也不去制止；道路上有饿死的人，您却不曾想到救济饥民。您真要想使国家强盛，就不要再发动战争，而把精力放在发展生产上，让老百姓有吃有穿，安居乐业，这样天下百姓都会来投奔您了。"

后来，人们引用"五十步笑百步"，比喻一个人的错误、缺点，其性质与别人一样，只是程度上轻一些，却去讥笑别人。

During the Warring States Period, because the Duke of Wei became over-confident in the power and prosperity of his state, he would often lead battles against the territories of the neighboring marquis. One day when Mencius went to see him, the duke said, "I have put my whole heart into running this country. When the Henei (present-day Jiyuan County in Henan Province) area was suffering from famine due to crop failures, I transported some of the famine victims to Hedong (present-day Anze County in Shanxi Province). At the same time, I also took the grain reserves at Hedong and allocated it to Henei to the relief of famine victims there. When Hedong was hit by a famine, I adopted the same measures. I once made an investigation of our neighboring states and have concluded that there is no king who takes care of the needs of his people like I do. Yet I don't understand why the population of the neighboring states does not decrease in number and the population of my country does not increase in number. Can you tell me the reason for this?"

Mencius replied, "Your Highness, since you are fond of warfare, I will use warfare as a metaphor to explain the reason to you. Amidst of the rattling of the battle drums and the clash of swords and spears, there will always be some cowardly soldiers who are afraid to die and throw down their helmets, armor, and weapons and flee in terror. Among these men, there will be those who in one breath run back 100 steps and those who run back 50 steps. The soldiers who ran back 50 steps will then jeer at those who ran back 100 steps, telling them how chicken-hearted they are. Do you think this is right?"

The King of Wei replied, "Of course not. Those who ran back 50 steps also retreated, the only difference is that they did not retreat by 100 steps, that is all."

Mencius said, "If Your Highness understand this story, then you should not complain that the population of your state is not growing. Though you have helped to provide some disaster relief for your people, you have not yet solved the basic subsistence problem plaguing your people as a whole. You often begin drafting men by force during seasons when farmers are planting crops or reaping the harvest. In this way you hold up the farming season and cause many fields to lie in waste. When the rich and powerful start to infringe upon the people's rights, you do nothing to stop them. Though the starving are all over the streets, you have never considered helping them. If you really want to see your country prosper, you must refrain from starting any more wars, and concentrate all your energy on developing your productivity, solving the basic subsistence problem for your people. Once your people can live and work in peace and contentment, then all people under heaven will seek refuge in your country."

The proverb "fifty steps laugh at 100 steps" means the person who is accusing someone else has made the same mistake or has the same shortcoming — though to a lesser degree — as the person he laughs at. The English equivalent of this proverb is "The pot calls the kettle black."

不 为 五 斗 米 折 腰

bú wèi wǔ dǒu mǐ zhé yāo

Refuse to bow down for 50 liters of rice

东晋著名诗人陶渊明年轻时曾希望能通过做官，实现他拯世救危、"佐君立业"的理想抱负。可是当他踏入官场以后，逐渐体察到统治阶级内部的卑鄙龌龊，社会政治的腐朽没落。认识到自己的想法错了。他不愿与作威作福，荒淫无耻的官僚们同流合污，时时打算退出污浊黑暗的官场。

陶渊明四十一岁那年，在彭泽县（今属江西省）当县令。一天，他正在处理公事，一名小吏进来报告说新任督邮大人来县视察，请他换上官服前去迎接。小吏告诉他，这新任督邮原是本县乡间富豪，靠着金钱贿赂，讨了个肥缺。此人卑劣无能，却喜欢装腔作势。陶渊明听了，不禁拍案而起，愤愤地说："我不能为五斗米的俸禄，向这种卑劣小人折腰！"说完，取出知县大印交给小吏，吩咐家人收拾行装，当即弃官而去。从此陶渊明再也没有做官，一直在乡间过着田园隐居生活。

后来，"不为五斗米折腰"被人们用来形容清高、有骨气，不为名利、富贵而向有权有势的人低头。

When the famous Eastern Han Dynasty poet Tao Yuanming was a young man, he dreamed that, by becoming an official and assisting the emperor in establishing his kingdom he could fulfil his goal of saving this troubled world. But after he stepped into the world of officialdom and gradually became aware of the sordid dealings within the ruling class and the corruption on the political scene, he realized that he was wrong. Not wanting to associate himself with the debauched bureaucrats who rode roughshod over the people, he was ready at any time to quit the dark and defiled officialdom.

At the age of 41, Tao became the magistrate of Pengze County (in present-day Jiangxi Province). One day, he was handling some official business when a lesser official came and informed him that the new government inspector was coming for an inspection, and he should change into his official clothes to go and welcome him. The lesser official then told him that the new inspector used to be a rich and powerful man in Pengze County, and it was through bribery that he had obtained the lucrative official post. He was an incompetent man with a mean character, who, nevertheless, loved to assume official airs. Tao Yuanming pounded the table, rose up, and angrily exclaimed, "I can't bow down to such a despicable rascal simply to earn my salary of 50 liters of rice!" Saying this, he took out his county seal, handed it to the lesser official, ordered his family members to pack his luggage, and immediately left his post. Henceforth, Tao never assumed another government office and spent the rest of his blissful days as a recluse in the countryside.

Later, the proverb "refuse to bow down for 50 liters of rice" is used to describe a man with moral integrity who stays aloof from personal fame and gain and refuses to bow to the rich and powerful.

不 敢 越 雷 池 一 步

bù gǎn yuè léi chí yí bù

No one step should be taken
beyond Leichi Lake

　　东晋时期，朝廷中有一位大臣名叫庾亮，是朝中掌握实权的显赫人物。公元327年，历阳内史苏峻和豫州史祖约以反对庾亮专权为名，起兵反晋。 叛军来势汹汹，直接进攻都城建康（今江苏南京市）。当时，庾亮的心腹大将温峤带兵镇守江州（今江西九江市一带）。 他得知消息后，心中非常焦急，准备亲自去建康援救。庾亮闻知，立即写了一封信，派快骑送给温峤，让他一定沉住气，不要离开战略要地江州。信中写道："吾忧西陲过于历阳，足下勿过雷池（湖泊名）一步也。"

　　温峤看信后，认识到自己的莽撞，就按庾亮的部署，仍旧驻扎江州。后来庾亮靠着温峤的军队，很快消灭了苏峻、祖约的叛军。

　　"不敢越雷池一步"后来用以比喻不敢或不要逾越一定的界限和范围。

During the Eastern Jin Dynasty (317–420), there was a court minister named Yu Liang, who was a man of real power and influence in his time. In 327, the chamberlain of Liyang, Su Jun, and the administrator of Yuzhou, Zu Yue, rose in armed rebellion against the Jin Dynasty under the pretext of opposing Yu's bid for political dominance. The rebel army came down with full force in a direct assault on the capital of Jiankang (present-day Nanjing in Jiangsu Province). When Yu Liang's trusted general, Wen Qiao, who was garrison commander in Jiangzhou (present-day Jiujiang, Jiangxi Province), heard about the revolt, he became very anxious, and decided to come personally to the rescue of Jiankang.

When Yu Liang learned about Wen Qiao's plan, he immediately wrote a letter to Wen and had it delivered to him by pony express. In the letter, he advised Wen to stay calm at all costs and not to leave Jiangzhou, a place of strategic importance. A line in the letter reads: "I am far more worried about the western border areas than Liyang. Please do not even make one step across Leichi Lake."

The letter brought home to Wen Qiao the danger of his impetuosity. He stayed at Jiangzhou just as Yu said. With the help of Wen Qiao's army, Yu Liang quickly put down the rebel forces of Su Jun and Zu Yue.

The proverb "no one step should be taken beyond Leichi Lake" later came to mean not to overstep certain prescribed boundaries and limits.

比 上 不 足　比 下 有 余

bǐ shàng bù zú　bǐ xià yǒu yú

Not up to those above,
but above those below

晋武帝司马炎在位时，朝廷中有位名叫王湛的官员。他满腹经纶，博学多闻，先后担任许多重要职务，但却曾经被人们当作傻子看待。

原来王湛自幼不爱讲话，但他极为聪慧，不仅有过目不忘的读书本领，而且看问题有独到的见解。只是他从不爱表现自己，因而知其才者甚少。

王湛有个侄子名叫王济。此人自恃有几分才气，瞧不起王湛。有一次王济有事到王湛房间去，看到王湛枕边有一本《周易》，就讥讽地问："你也用得着这本书吗？"遂让王湛讲解一二。王湛并不理会，当即滔滔不绝地讲了起来。他先谈《周易》的内容旨意，又条分缕析，阐述其玄理妙道。王济不禁对叔父肃然起敬。他一连在叔父房里请教了几天，越加感到叔父的学问精深，说："家有名士，三十年而不知，我真是愚蠢啊！"

一天，晋武帝见到王济，问起他的痴叔。王济说："臣叔其实不痴。"接着就把王湛的才识介绍了一遍。武帝听了也很吃惊，说："依你看来他可以和谁相比？"王济答道："山涛以下，魏舒以上。"后来，人们一提到王湛，都称他"上比山涛不足，下比魏舒有余*。"

后来，此语演变为"比上不足，比下有余"，用以说明比胜

68

于自己的差一些，比不如自己的好一些。常作自谦语使用。

*山涛、魏舒：均为汉武帝时的名臣。

During the reign of Emperor Wu Di of the Western Jin Dynasty (265–316), there was a courtier named Wang Zhan. Though he was rather knowledgeable and well-versed in state craft, having assumed many important state offices, he once was looked upon as a simpleton.

It turned out that since childhood Wang Zhan had been a reticent yet extremely bright boy. Not only did he possess a photographic memory when it came to reading books, but he also had an original approach to various issues. Because he never liked to show off, however, his talents remained virtually unknown.

Wang Zhan had a nephew named Wang Ji. Because he had an overrated view of his own talent, he looked down on Wang Zhan. Once, Wang Ji had to see Wang Zhan about something and noticed that Wang Zhan had a copy of *I-Ching (the Book of Changes)* next to his pillow. He jeered at Wang Zhan, "What use do you have of this book?" He then asked him for a simple explanation of its content. Wang Zhan did not really pay attention to what he said and immediately started talking non-stop about the book. He first began by discussing the content and central idea of the book, and then continued with a line-by-line exposition of the text, expounding upon some of the most mysterious and profound portions of the book. Wang Ji could not help but be filled with a deep admiration for his uncle. After consulting his uncle at his house for several days on end, he became even more impressed with his uncle's broad range of knowledge and profound scholarship. He exclaimed, "Truly our family has produced a man of renown, and yet for 30 years I was not aware of this. Oh, how foolish I have been!"

One day, Emperor Wu Di met Wang Ji and asked about his uncle the simpleton. Wang Ji replied, "My uncle is actually no simpleton at all." He then went on to explain the genius of his uncle to the emperor. The emperor, astounded, said, "In your eyes, who do you think is his equal?" Wang Ji replied, "He is below Shan Tao, yet above Wei Shu."* Later, whenever people mentioned Wang Zhan, they would say, "He is not as bright as Shan Tao but brighter than Wei Shu."

Later this proverb evolved into "not up to those above, but above those below," which means one will always be a little worse off than those who are better, but always a little better than those who are worse. It is often used as an expression of self-humility.

---

* Shan Tao and Wei Shu were both famous officials during the reign of Emperor Wu Di of the Western Han Dynasty.

以小人之心 度君子之腹

yǐ xiǎo rén zhī xīn duó jūn zǐ zhī fù

Thinking like a petty man
to judge the intentions of a gentleman

春秋时候，晋国的梗阳县发生了一起民事纠纷。由于案子比较复杂，梗阳大夫魏戊就把案件上报给国相魏舒审理。诉讼人为了打赢官司，就向魏舒行贿，送给他几位能歌善舞的美女。魏舒动了心，打算收下来。魏戊知道这件事后，要大夫阎没和女宽设法劝阻魏舒。

　　这天退朝以后，阎没和女宽来到魏舒家中，正赶上吃饭的时候，魏舒留下他们一块用餐。当酒菜还没有摆好时，两个大夫一连几次摇头叹气。吃完饭以后，魏舒便问他们为何叹气。两个人赶忙回答说："昨天没有吃晚饭，非常饿，所以饭菜刚端上来，我们恐怕不够吃，就禁不住叹气。饭菜上了一半，我们就责备自己说：'难道国相请我们吃饭会不够吃？'因此再次叹气。等到丰盛的菜上完，我们更加感到刚才的想法不对，是以小人只想吃饱肚子的想法去揣测君子的内心，一个人原应当知足才好啊！"魏舒听了，知道两位大夫是在劝阻自己：不要为贪图享受而受贿。于是便拒绝了诉讼人送来的美女。

　　后来从这个故事演变出"以小人之心，度君子之腹"，这个谚语，用来形容以小人卑劣的想法去揣测道德品行高尚的人的动机。

During the Spring and Autumn Period, a civil dispute arose in Gengyang County in the State of Jin. Because of the complexity of the case, Wei Wu, a senior official from Gengyang, turned over the case to the State Counselor Wei Shu. In order to win the lawsuit, the plaintiff offered to bribe Wei Shu with a few beautiful sing-song girls. The temptation was so irresistible that Wei Shu wanted to accept it. When Wei Wu knew about this, he called on other two officials Yan Mo and Nu Kuan to do all they could to dissuade Wei Shu.

One day, after Yan Mo and Nu Kuan left the court after an audience with the duke, they went to Wei Shu's home. It was lunch time, and Wei Shu invited them to stay for lunch with him. Before all the dishes were laid out on the table, the two men kept shaking their heads and sighing. After the meal, Wei Shu asked them why they were sighing. The two immediately responded, "Yesterday we didn't eat and so we were starving today. When the food arrived, we were afraid we wouldn't get enough to eat, so we started sighing. After half the dishes had arrived, we began to blame ourselves: 'Is it possible that the State Counselor would invite us to lunch but give us not enough to eat?' That's why we were sighing. But after all the dishes were served, we felt that we were wrong to misunderstand you. We were so eager to fill our stomachs that we were thinking like petty men to gauge the heart and intentions of a gentleman. It is far better for a person to learn self-contentment!" At these words, Wei Shu knew that they had come to exhort him not to take a bribe just for the sake of personal enjoyment. He thus refused the plaintiff's offer of beautiful girls.

Later the proverb "thinking like a petty man to judge the intentions of a gentleman" came to mean that one uses the base thinking of a petty person to guess the intentions of a man of noble character.

以 貌 取 人 失 之 子 羽

yǐ mào qǔ rén shī zhī zǐ yǔ

Judging a talent solely by his appearance is doing him an injustice

春秋时期，孔子有个得意弟子名叫澹台灭明，字子羽。他相貌生得粗壮丑陋。孔子刚见到他时，很是瞧不起他，觉得他不是读书的材料。子羽再三请求，孔子才勉强收下他做自己的学生。子羽决心改变老师对自己的看法。平时没有事情，他决不出门，整日躲在书房里发奋苦读。他还注意自己的道德修养，处处按老师的教导去做。这样不到三年，子羽的德行、学问都高出其他同学。

学成之后，子羽告别老师到南方吴国游学。在那里，他设立学馆，广招门徒，先后有三百余人随他学习，广泛地传播了中原文化和儒家思想。孔子听到子羽取得的成绩后，十分感慨，说："我仅凭言语鉴别人才，在宰予*身上犯了过失；我仅凭外貌衡量人才，在子羽身上犯了过失。"

后来，人们引用"以貌取人，失之子羽"来比喻单凭相貌选取人才，是会犯错误的。

*宰予：孔子的弟子，曾因不同意孔子的有些主张而受到孔子的批评。

During the Spring and Autumn Period, Confucius was extremely pround of a disciple of his named Tantai Mieming. Tantai Mieming, with the style name Zi Yu, was ugly and coarse in appearance. At the first sight of him, Confucius looked down upon him, deeming him unsuitable for learning. It was only at Zi Yu's repeated requests that Confucius reluctantly accepted him as his pupil. From then on, Zi Yu was determined to change his teacher's bias towards him. Unless there was something important, he would stay indoors the whole day studying and reading. He also concentrated on moral cultivation, strictly adhering to the instructions of his teacher. In less than three years, Zi Yu greatly exceeded his fellow schoolmates in moral and academic achievements.

After graduation, Zi Yu bid farewell to his teacher and promoted Confucian theories in the State of Wu in the south of China. He established an academy and took in as many students as possible. Altogether, there were over three hundred people who studied there. Because of his school, the culture of Central Plains and Confucian theories were disseminated far and wide. The great achievement of Zi Yu impressed Confucius deeply. "Judging people solely by their speech, I have done wrong to Zai Yu (one of his disciples who had been criticized for holding a different opinion); selecting talents only by their appearance, I have done injustice to Zi Yu," he said, sighing.

Later, people cite Confucius' words to emphasize that one will certainly make a mistake if one determines talent only based on a person's outward appearance.

未 知 鹿 死 谁 手
wèi zhī lù sǐ shuí shǒu

It's still hard to tell
at whose hand the deer will die

东晋时期，北方匈奴、鲜卑、氐(dī)、羌、羯(jié)五个少数民族，先后建立了十六个国家。其中羯族建立的政权史称"后赵"，开国皇帝是石勒。石勒出身于贫苦人家，小时候做过商贩，也给富人当过长工。后来他参加了刘渊的反晋部队，被拜为大将。公元319年，石勒起兵反对刘曜的前赵政权，自立为帝。由于他的才干和苦心经营，后赵占领了北方的大部份地区，成为诸国中最强大的一个国家。

对于自己建立的功业，石勒非常得意。在一次宴会上，他乘着酒兴问大臣徐光："我和自古以来的开国君主相比，怎么样呢？"善于逢迎拍马的徐光马上回答说："陛下的文韬武略超过汉高祖刘邦、魏武帝曹操。自三皇五帝以来，没有谁能比得上您。您可以说是轩辕皇帝*第二。"石勒倒是很有自知之明，他笑着说："你说得太过分了，如果我出生在汉高祖时，我甘愿做他的臣子，假如我与汉光武帝刘秀生在同一时代，我一定同他在中原大地较量一下，还未知鹿死谁手呢！"我的能耐在于刘邦、刘秀之间，哪里能与轩辕皇帝相比呢！"

文武百官听了都高呼"万岁"。徐光则脸上红一阵，白一阵，好不尴尬。

后来，"未知鹿死谁手"演变成谚语。古人常以鹿比喻帝位和国家政权，因此此谚语旧时用以形容天下不知将被谁夺得；现在则多指体育比赛中势均力敌的双方，争夺激烈，胜败难以预料。

*轩辕皇帝：即黄帝，传说中的上古圣明帝王。

During the Eastern Jin Dynasty, five ethnic groups in the northern part of China including the Xiongnu, Xianbei, Di, Qiang and Jie established 16 states successively. Of these political powers, the Jie regime was called Later Zhao State by historians. Their founder was Shi Le. Born into a poor family, Shi Le made a living as a vendor in his childhood and served as a farmhand for the rich. Later, he joined the anti-Jin army led by Liu Yuan (founder of the State of Han) and was appointed as general. In the year 319, he rose in rebellion against the former Zhao State established by Liu Yao, a nephew of Liu Yuan, and proclaimed himself an emperor. Due to his talent and efforts, the Later Zhao swept most of the northern area, becoming the most powerful state.

Shi Le was rather proud of his exploits. Once after a few drinks at a banquet, he asked Minister Xu Guang, "How do I compare with those ancient state founders?" Xu Guang, known as a sycophant, readily answered, "Your Majesty, your literary attainments and military strategy have greatly exceeded that of Liu Bang, founder of the Western Han Dynasty, and Cao Cao, founder of the Kingdom of Wei during the Three Kingdoms Period. You are unrivaled ever since the time of the legendary Three Kings and Five Emperors. It's no exaggeration to say that you are the second legendary Huang Di (Yellow Emperor)." However, Shi Le kept a sober mind and retorted, "You must be flattering me. If I had lived in the time of the Western Han Dynasty, I would have very willingly served Liu Bang as a subordinate; if I were a contemporary with Liu Xiu, founder of the Eastern Han Dynasty, I would have contested with him in the Central Plains. But it's still hard to tell at whose hand the deer will die! I reckon that my ability is between that of Liu Bang and Liu Xiu, but falls largely behind that of Huang Di."

All the officials present applauded, "Long live Your Majesty!" leaving Xu Guang in a state of embarrassment. Gradually, "it's still hard to tell at whose hand the deer will die" developed into a proverb. In ancient times, the word "deer" also had the meaning of emperorship and political power. Therefore, the original phrase implied that no one knew who would get command of the entire world. Nowadays, this saying is often applied to describe the difficulty of predicting the final outcome between two closely-matched competitors in a physical contest.

巧 妇 难 为 无 米 之 炊

qiǎo fù nán wéi wú mǐ zhī chuī

Even the cleverest housewife can't cook a meal without rice

宋代时候，有个名叫晏景初的尚书。有一次，他领着一班人马出门办事，到了傍晚没能赶回城里，只好到野外的一座寺庙里请求僧人让他们住上一宿。庙里的僧人推辞说，庙里很穷，空闲的房舍不多，而且又太简陋，无法安排这么多贵客。晏景初讥讽说："有才能的人解决这么点小事是很容易的。"僧人反驳说："如果没有米，即便是巧媳妇又怎么能煮出饭来呢?"

　　"巧妇难为无米之炊"是一条古老的谚语，用来比喻能力再强，缺少必要条件也办不成事。

During the Song Dynasty (960–1279), there lived a senior official called Yan Jingchu. Once, he led his entourage on a trip to handle business and was unable to make it back to the city by evening. They had to find accommodations in a temple in the country. However, one of the monks refused them, explaining that they were rather poor, had only few vacant rooms, and even those empty rooms were simple and crude, not suitable for distinguished guests. Hearing the monk's excuse, Yan Jingchu retorted ironically, "In my opinion, it's a piece of cake for a talented man like me to solve such trifles." "That's right," the monk argued, "But even the cleverest housewife can't cook a meal without rice."

Now people cite this old proverb "even the cleverest housewife can't cook a meal without rice" to show that no matter how capable a man is, if he is not provided with the necessary conditions, he will achieve nothing.

四 海 之 内 皆 兄 弟

sì hǎi zhī nèi jiē xiōng dì

Within the four seas all men are brothers

春秋时候，孔子的学生司马牛，为人忠厚正派，可是他的兄长和几个弟弟却都不安分守己。特别是他的长兄桓魋，阴险奸诈，靠着逢迎奉承骗得了宋国国君的宠信，却又暗中与自己的兄弟阴谋反叛。司马牛极力劝阻他们，他们根本不听。后来国君觉察到桓的阴谋，派兵打败了他们。桓魋和他的几个兄弟，有的被杀，有的逃亡。司马牛为此受到株连，不敢在宋国再呆下去，也逃到了国外。

　　司马牛在国外四处流浪。他常常为自家兄弟的行为感到羞愧，又为自己孑然一身而伤心。有一次，司马牛见到同学子夏，忧心忡忡地对他说："别人都有好兄弟，唯独我没有。"子夏开导他说："君子敬而无失，与人恭而有礼，四海之内，皆兄弟也。"（意思是说：君子只要做事严肃认真，不出差错，待人谦恭有礼，那么，天下的人都是他的好兄弟。）司马牛听了，感到有道理，从此就不再感到愁苦和孤单了。

　　后来，人们引用"四海之内皆兄弟"说明普天下人都是兄弟，应友好相处。

During the Spring and Autumn Period, there was a disciple of Confucius named Sima Niu, who led an honest and noble life. His brothers, however, did not behave themselves, especially his elder brother, Huan Tui, was sinister and fraudulent. He wormed himself into the duke of Song's confidence by way of flattery, while conspiring with the other brothers against the duke. Sima Niu tried his best to stop them, but to no avail. Later, the duke got word of their intrigue and sent troops to deal with them. As a result, some of them were killed and others fled away. Because of this incident, Sima Niu no longer dared to stay in the State of Song and became a fugitive abroad.

As a wanderer in a foreign country, Sima Niu often felt shame for the misbehavior of his brothers and sad for his loneliness as well. Once, he met Zi Xia, another disciple of Confucius and told him about his worries, sighing, "Everyone has good brothers except me." Zi Xia comforted him by saying, "Within the four seas all men are brothers so long as one takes a serious attitude towards one's work and treats others politely." Sima Niu followed Zi Xia's suggestion and from that day on, never felt depressed or lonely anymore.

Later, people cite the proverb "within the four seas all men are brothers" to imply that all men all over the world born equal, and therefore should live in harmony.

瓜 田 不 纳 履 李 下 不 整 冠

guā tián bú nà lǚ lǐ xià bù zhěng guān

Never pull on your shoes in a melon patch; never adjust your cap under a plum tree

唐文宗李昂派一名叫郭旻（mín）的大臣去做邠宁（今陕西彬县）的地方长官。这件事情在朝廷内外引起议论。人们说这是因为郭旻进献了两个女儿入宫，才得到这个官职的。唐文宗听到这种议论后，十分生气，他对工部侍郎柳公权说：“郭旻做官一向不曾有过什么过失，把他放在邠宁做地方官，实在不算什么。再说他的两个女儿进宫是侍候太后的，同我丝毫没有关系呀！”柳公权说：“瓜田李下的嫌疑，怎么能够给每户人家都解释清楚呢？”唐文宗听了也感到毫无办法。

　　柳公权所说的“瓜李之嫌”，就是从“瓜田不纳履，李下不整冠”两句话压缩而来的。这两句话出自古乐府诗《君子行》中：

　　君子防未然，不处嫌疑间；

　　瓜田不纳履，李下不整冠。

　　后来，这两句诗被人们作为谚语使用，比喻做事应该避嫌以免招惹麻烦。

During the Tang Dynasty, Emperor Wen Zong appointed Minister Guo Min as the magistrate of Binning around present-day Binxian County in Shaanxi Province. The news aroused a heated discussion both in the court and in the public. Rumor had it that the reason why Guo Min obtained the position was because he had offered two of his daughters to the imperial family. Having learned of this unfounded rumor, Emperor Wen Zong got angry, saying to Liu Gongquan, Minister of Works, "Guo Min has never done anything wrong in his career, and it's only natural for me to put him in charge of Binning. Moreover, his two daughters are sent to serve my mother, which has nothing to do with me!" "But the suspicion aroused in a melon patch or under a plum tree is still there," Liu Gongquan answered. "How can you convince everyone?" Upon hearing Liu's words, Emperor Wen Zong realized that he could do nothing more to stop the talk of the town.

"The suspicion aroused in a melon patch or under a plum tree" is the short of "never pull on your shoes in a melon patch; never adjust your cap under a plum tree" which is taken from the *Song of Gentleman*, an ancient folk song. The story says that a gentleman should always avoid suspicion, never pulling on his shoes in a melon patch or adjusting his cap under a plum tree.

Gradually, these lines were used as a proverb to remind people that avoiding suspicion may help one avoid later troubles.

宁 为 玉 碎　不 为 瓦 全

nìng wéi yù suì　bù wéi wǎ quán

**Rather be a shattered vessel of
jade than an unbroken piece of pottery**

南北朝时期，战乱不断，统治阶级内部为争权夺利，互相残杀。公元550年，东魏大将高洋废掉魏孝静帝元善见，建立了北齐政权，并自立为帝（齐文宣帝）。他残酷打击异己，大肆屠杀元氏家族的人，前后杀死七百余人。当时有个叫元景安的人，为了讨好皇帝，免遭杀戮，奏请皇帝改姓高。可是他的堂兄元景皓表示坚决反对，说："岂得弃本宗，逐他姓？大丈夫宁可玉碎，不能瓦全！"元景安把元景皓的这些话报告了高洋，结果元景皓被杀，其家属被流放到远方。元景安得皇帝准许，遂改姓高，受到了奖赏，以后还做了高官。

　　后来，人们把"宁可玉碎，不能瓦全"说作"宁为玉碎，不为瓦全"，比喻宁可为正义的事业壮烈牺牲，也不愿丧失气节，苟且偷生。

The Northern and Southern Dynasties were a time of endless wars and chaos. Different groups of the ruling class fought with each other to gain more political and financial power. In 550, General Gao Yang of the Eastern Wei dethroned Emperor Xiao Jing (Yuan Shanjian) and established the Northern Qi Dynasty. He proclaimed himself Emperor Wen Xuan. He attacked his political opponents and mercilessly murdered the members of the Yuan family. More than seven hundreds people were slaughtered. At that time there was a man called Yuan Jing'an who pled for permission to change his surname to Gao so as to avoid persecution and ingratiate himself with Emperor Wen Xuan. However, Yuan Jinghao, his cousin on the paternal side, was strongly against this and rebuked him, "How can you abandon your family name for another one? A real man would rather die like a shattered vessel of jade than drag out a humiliated existence like an unbroken piece of pottery." Yuan Jing'an reported to the emperor of what his cousin had said. Consequently, Yuan Jinghao was killed, and the rest of his family were sent into faraway exile. Yuan Jing'an was permitted to change his surname to Gao and got a reward before becoming a senior official.

People of later generations cite this saying to show that they would rather die in glory than live in dishonor.

司马昭之心　路人皆知

sī mǎ zhāo zhī xīn　lù rén jiē zhī

Sima Zhao's ill intent is known to all

　　三国时，魏明帝死后，年幼的曹芳继位，由开国功臣司马懿辅政。从此魏国的大权落入司马氏手中，魏国皇帝只徒有其名了。后来，司马懿死后，他的儿子司马师废掉曹芳，另换十三岁的曹髦为帝。司马师死后，他的弟弟司马昭又继续执掌魏国军政大权。

　　司马昭总揽大权后，野心更大，总想取代曹髦，自己做皇帝；因此不断剪除异己，打击政敌。年轻的曹髦知道自己即便做"傀儡"皇帝也休想当长，迟早会被司马昭除去，就打算铤而走险，用突然袭击的办法，干掉司马昭。

　　一天，他把跟随自己的心腹大臣找来，对他们说："司马昭之心，路人皆知也。吾不能坐受废辱，今日当与卿自出讨之。"

　　几位大臣知道这样做无异于飞蛾投火，就劝他暂时忍耐。可曹髦不听，亲自率领左右仆从、侍卫数百人去袭击司马昭。谁知大臣中早有人把这消息报告了司马昭。司马昭立即派兵阻截，把曹髦杀掉了。

　　后来，人们用"司马昭之心，路人皆知"来比喻阴谋野心已为人所共知。

During the Three Kingdoms period, after the death of Cao Rui, Emperor Ming Di of the Kingdom of Wei, the young Cao Fang succeeded to the throne, with Sima Yi, one of the state-founders, as his assistant. It was then that the power in the kingdom fell into the hands of the Sima family and the emperor became a mere puppet. Later, when Sima Yi died, his son Sima Shi dethroned Cao Fang and established Cao Mao as the emperor. When Sima Shi died, his younger brother Sima Zhao continued to wield military and political control over Wei.

As powerful as he was, Sima Zhao still was not satisfied. Determined to usurp Cao Mao and become the new emperor, Sima Zhao constantly eliminated dissenters and attacked all his political opponents. Cao Mao knew that his days as a puppet emperor were numbered and sooner or later he would be replaced by Sima Zhao. Therefore, Cao Mao determined to take a risk and attempt to get rid of Sima Zhao by a sudden raid.

One day, Cao Mao summoned his trusted ministers and said, "Sima Zhao's vicious intent is known to all. I don't want to be humiliated without doing anything. Today I shall go fighting him with all of you."

Realizing that this rash decision was nothing but a moth darting into a flame, his ministers persuaded Cao Mao to be patient and wait for the time, but to no avail. With hundreds of followers and soldiers, Cao Mao led a raid upon Sima Zhao. But little did he know that one of his own ministers had already tipped Sima Zhao, and Cao Mao was assassinated on his way to attack Sima Zhao.

Nowadays, people use the saying "Sima Zhao's ill intent is known to all" to indicate a malicious conspiracy which has become public knowledge.

民 以 食 为 天

mín yǐ shí wéi tiān

People can't do without enough food

公元前 204 年夏天，楚王项羽挥师攻打汉王刘邦，一下子攻占了战略重地荥（xíng）阳（今河南荥阳）、成皋（今河南荥阳东北）。在项羽强大的攻势下，刘邦仓皇失措，准备抛弃成皋以东的地盘，向西撤退。

刘邦有一个谋臣，名叫郦食其。他仔细分析了当时的形势，认为这样做对汉军十分不利。他又打听到项羽屯积粮草的重地敖仓，没有多少兵力把守，感到有机可乘。于是就找到刘邦献计说："王者以民为天，而民以食为天。"敖仓这个地方，储藏着楚军的大批粮食，而守兵却很少。只要我们攻取敖仓，然后下决心夺回荥阳、成皋；老百姓见我们粮草丰足，又占据险要之地，就会归顺我们。这样还愁打不败项羽吗？"

刘邦听从了这个建议，马上派兵攻取了敖仓，使军心大振，很快扭转了不利的战局。

后来，人们引用"民以食为天"，来说明人民把吃饭问题看作是最重要的。

In the summer of 204 B.C., Xiang Yu, the lord of Chu (present-day Hubei Province) commanded an army to attack Liu Bang, the lord of Han (present-day Sichuan and Shaanxi provinces). In no time he took two fortresses, namely Xingyang (northeast to present-day Xingyang in Henan Province) and Chenggao (northwest to present-day Xingyang). The onslaught threw Liu Bang into a panic. He even thought of abandoning the area east of Chenggao and retreating to the west.

After a close analysis of the situation, Li Yiji, a military counselor, held that Liu Bang's decision would put the army of Han in a vulnerable position. Having heard that Aocang, a major granary for Xiang Yu, was poorly guarded, Li Yiji decided that this was an opportunity he could take advantage of. He came to Liu Bang with this advice: "I've heard that the king can't do without his people, while people can't do without enough food. Since most of the grain provisions for the army of Chu is stored at Aocang and the granary is poorly protected, we can capture it and go on to take back Xingyang and Chenggao. When the citizens find that we have plenty of food and occupied such important fortresses, they will obey us. Then what fear is there of not being able to defeat Xiang Yu?"

Accepting Li Yiji's suggestion, Liu Bang dispatched his troops and seized Aocang immediately. The victory boosted the morale of Liu's army and turned the tables.

Later, people quote the saying "people can't do without enough food" to explain the fact that people regard food as their most important need.

百 闻 不 如 一 见

bǎi　wén　bù　rú　yí　jiàn

Seeing once is better than hearing for a hundred times

战国时期，魏文侯派西门豹去治理邺（yè）地（今河北省临漳县西）。临走时，魏文侯反复交代西门豹，到了邺地，处理事情，一定要亲自调查研究后再作出决定，不能轻信传闻和官吏的汇报。他说："夫耳闻之，不如目见之；目见之，不如足践之；足践之，不如手辨之。人始入官，如入晦室，久而愈明，明乃治，治乃行。"这段话的意思是，耳朵听到不如亲眼看到，亲眼看到不如实地调查，实地调查不如仔细分析，辨别真伪。一个人开始做官时，就像突然走进暗室里一样，过了很久，眼睛才能明亮，只有眼睛明亮了，才能辨别事物，才能治理国事。

　　西门豹到了邺地以后，遵照魏文侯的嘱咐，深入到民间，了解老百姓的疾苦。通过调查，他得知当地乡绅、巫婆利用水灾敲诈和危害百姓的罪行，就采取严厉措施，对他们狠狠打击。同时，西门豹还组织老百姓开凿水渠，变水害为水利，发展了农业生产。没过多久，邺地很快被西门豹治理成为富饶、安定的地区。

　　"耳闻不如目见"后来演变为"百闻不如一见"。这一谚语告诉人们，耳听为虚，眼见为实，凡事要调查研究才能下结论。

During the Warring States Period, Duke Wen Hou of the State of Wei appointed Ximen Bao the magistrate of Ye (west of present-day Linzhang in Hebei Province). On departure, Wen Hou repeatedly exhorted Ximen Bao to make decisions only after he had personally made investigation and analysis, instead of giving ready credence to rumors or official reports. "Seeing it for yourself is better than hearing it from others. However, on-the-spot investigation is better than just seeing it, and careful analysis is still better than investigation," Wen Hou said. "To begin an official career is like entering a dark room all of a sudden. Gradually, your eyes grow accustomed to the darkness, enabling you to see things more and more clearly. Only then can you take correct and effective measures."

When Ximen Bao arrived at Ye, he adhered to the duke's words and went among the local people to know about their plight. Having learned that the local gentry and witches were taking advantage of the flood to extort money from the residents, he took strict measures to crack down on all of them. Meanwhile, he organized the local people to dig canals, thereby turning the scourge of excessive water into a blessing. As a result, agricultural production boomed. Under Ximen Bao's administration, the place soon became a prosperous and peaceful land.

This story gave rise to the saying "seeing once is better than hearing for a hundred times," which emphasizes the importance of investigation and analysis. It is always more reliable to depend on one's eyesight than on hearsay.

百尺竿头 更进一步

bǎi chǐ gān tóu gèng jìn yí bù

**Make further progress even if
you've come a long way**

北宋时候，有一位很有名气的佛家大师名叫招贤。有一次，一个和尚向招贤请教关于佛教修行的问题。招贤随口说了几句诗送给他："百尺竿头*不动人，虽然得入未为真；百尺竿头须进步，十方世界**是全身。"这几句诗的意思是：修行即便到了百尺竿头这样高的境界，也不应该满足，还要继续努力。这样就可以与整个宇宙浑然一体，达到无所不至的境界。

后来，"百尺竿头须进步"这一佛家语，演变作"百尺竿头，更进一步"这条谚语，用来比喻即使取得了很大的成绩，也不能自满自足，仍要不断前进。

*百尺竿头：佛教语，用以比喻修行到了极高的境界。
**十方世界：佛教用以指整个宇宙空间。

During the Northern Song Dynasty (960–1127), there lived a famous Buddhist named Zhao Xian. Once, a monk consulted him on Buddhist self-cultivation. Zhao Xian answered casually, "You should not be complacent when you've come a long way in self-cultivation, for you haven't attained the essence of Buddhism yet; you've got to work harder, until you become one with the universe."

Later, these encouraging words developed into the saying "Make further progress even if you've come a long way."

有 则 改 之　无 则 加 勉

yǒu zé gǎi zhī　wú zé jiā miǎn

Correct mistakes if you've committed them, and guard against them if you have not

104

春秋时，孔子的得意门生曾参非常注意自己的道德行为修养，处处严格要求自己，因此经常受到孔子的称赞。孔子的其他弟子便去向曾参请教如何修养身心，成为品行高尚的人。曾参说："吾日三省吾身：为人谋而不忠乎？与朋友交而不信乎？传不习乎？"（意思是：我每天多次反省自己：替朋友办事尽心尽力了吗？与朋友往来诚实吗？老师传授我的知识复习了吗？）前来求教的人听了，内心都很佩服，说："我们一定向您学习，按您所说的去做。"

宋代朱熹在《朱子全书·论语》中，对曾参这段话作了注释："曾子以此三者省其身，有则改之，无则加勉。"（意思是：曾参常就以上三个方面检查自己，有缺点就改正，没有就用来勉励自己。）

后来，人们引用"有则改之，无则加勉"来说明要正确对待别人的批评，如确有错误就改正，如没有就努力避免它。

During the Spring and Autumn Period, Zeng Shen, one of Confucius' favorite disciples, attached great importance to the cultivation of moral behavior, putting strict demands on himself in all respects. Since he was often highly-praised by his teacher the other disciples went to consult him on self-cultivation in the hope of becoming a man of virtue. Zeng Shen told them, "Everyday I asked myself these three questions: Have I done my best to help others? Have I been true and honest when associating with my friends? Have I reviewed what I have learned from the teacher?" His listeners said to him with deep admiration, "We are determined to follow your example."

Zhu Xi, a famous philosopher and educator in the Southern Song Dynasty (1127–1279), gave an explanation to Zeng Shen's words in his book *A Complete Collection of Zhu Zi's Works*: "Using these three criteria to judge himself, Zeng Shen would correct his mistakes if he had made them and guard against them if he hadn't."

This saying was cited to encourage people to take a correct attitude towards criticism.

有其父必有其子

yǒu qí fù bì yǒu qí zǐ

Like father, like son

战国时期，齐国人尹文有个儿子很愚笨，因此他总怀疑这孩子不是自己的亲生子，常常用木棍、皮鞭毒打他。

　　有一天，孔子的孙子子思来到尹文家中拜访。恰值尹文正为儿子的事气恼，见子思来了就气冲冲地说："这个孩子肯定不是我的儿子。我一直怀疑我的妻子不贞洁，大概是她和别人私通生的。所以我决定把妻子休掉！"子思说："如果像您所说的那样，那么尧和舜（传说中上古时代的贤明君主）的妻子是否贞洁也值得怀疑。尧、舜两位圣君是那样地英明，可他们的儿子丹朱和商均的道德、才能却连一般的老百姓都不如。按您的逻辑推断，丹朱和商均怎么会是尧和舜的儿子呢？'有此父斯有此子，道之常也。'（有这样的父亲，就会有这样的儿子。这句话说的是通常的道理。）倘若贤明的父亲生了愚昧的儿子，这也是很自然的现象，决不是妻子的罪过。"子思还要说下去，被尹文打断了。"先生请不要再讲了，道理我已明白，我不会再赶走妻子了。"

　　后来，"有此父斯有此子"演变为"有其父必有其子"，用以说明父亲的言行对孩子有很大的影响，因此孩子常常在某些方面像父亲。

In the Warring States Period, there was a man named Yin Wen in the State of Qi. Yin had a very stupid son and he suspected that the child was not his own. To give vent to his anger, Yin often beat the child.

One day, Confucius' grandson Zi Si came to visit Yin Wen and found him at his son. Yin said, "This kid cannot be my son. I have been suspecting that my wife had an affair with somebody else and this kid must be the result of her adultery. So I have made up my mind to divorce her!" Zi Si replied, "If that is the case then we should also suspect the virtue of the wives of Yao and Shun.* Both Yao and Shun were famous sages but their sons were not so capable and respectable as commoners. According to your logic, how could Yao and Shun have such sons? Like father, like son — I know this is common sense. But it is natural that a smart father has a stupid son. Definitely, that is not your wife's fault...." Yin interrupted Zi Si, "Master, I understand what you mean. I now know it's my fault and I promise that I will not blame my wife any more."

The proverb "like father, like son" means that because the father has great influence upon the son, so the son will take after his father in many respects.

---

* Yao and Shun are legendary monarchs of ancient China.

成也萧何 败也萧何

chéng yě xiāo hé   bài yě xiāo hé

Success or failure,
Xiao He is the man behind it

秦朝末年，有位淮阴人士叫韩信。他精于谋略，擅长用兵，很有军事才能。起初，他在项羽部下做一名小军官，几次向项羽出谋献计，均未被采纳。于是韩信便逃到与项羽争夺天下的刘邦那里。可是刘邦也不重用他，委任的官职还不如先前高呢！韩信感到在刘邦这里仍然无法施展抱负，整日闷闷不乐，准备另投他处。

　　就在这时，韩信偶然见到了刘邦的丞相萧何。经过交谈，萧何感到韩信是个难得的将才，便答应在刘邦面前举荐他。可是过了好久不见回音，韩信就找个机会逃走了。萧何听说韩信逃走，心急如焚，来不及向刘邦说明情况，就去追赶；一直追了两天，才把韩信追回来。刘邦见萧何如此器重韩信，便接受了建议，提拔韩信为统帅各路兵马的大将军。

　　从此以后，韩信为刘邦东征西战，几年功夫，便攻下了许多诸侯国；垓下一战，又把项羽彻底消灭，使刘邦占有了天下。建立了汉朝。

　　刘邦做了皇帝以后，却对韩信猜忌起来。先是突然解除了他的兵权，不久又以谋反的罪名把他逮捕，赦免后降封为淮阴侯。后来，韩信被告发谋反。当时刘邦不在京城，刘邦的妻子吕后就找来担任丞相的萧何商量。萧何设计将韩信骗入宫中，以谋反罪名把他杀害了。

　　这个历史故事演变出"成也萧何，败也萧何"这句谚语，用以比喻事情的成败都是由一个人造成的。

Towards the end of the Qin Dynasty (221–207 B.C.), there was a man named Han Xin from Huaiyin near present-day Huaiyin, Jiangsu Province. Han Xin was a very brave man and well-versed in the art of war, but he was just a minor officer under Xiang Yu who was vying for national power with Liu Bang. His strategic advice having been repeatedly rejected by Xiang Yu, Han Xin went to Xiang Yu's opponent Liu Bang, only to see that Liu Bang did not think highly of him either. Being assigned to an even lower post than before, Han Xin concluded that he could not realize his ambition under Liu Bang either so he became very depressed and began to think about crossing over to someone else.

At this moment, Han Xin met Xiao He, Liu Bang's prime minister. After a conversation with Han Xin, Xiao He felt that Han Xin was an exceptional talent and promised to recommend him to Liu Bang. But after Han Xin did not hear from Xiao He for a long time, he thought Liu Bang did not take him seriously, and ran away. The news caused much anxiety in Xiao He. Without so much as to report to Liu Bang, he went to chase after Han Xin. After a pursuit of two days, he brought Han Xin back. Seeing that Xiao He thought so highly of Han Xin, Liu Bang accepted Xiao He's suggestion and promoted Han Xin to be a high-ranking general. From that time on, Han Xin fought countless battles for Liu Bang, took many states, wiped out Xiang Yu's army in the Gaixia Battle,* thereby enabling Liu Bang to unify the country and establish the Han Dynasty.

But after Liu Bang took the throne he began to have suspicion against Han Xin. Soon Han Xin was relieved of his military power and was then arrested on charges of treason. When he was released on special pardon, he was made Duke of Huaiyin. But that did not last long, and soon report came that Han Xin was plotting a mutiny. At that time Liu Bang was not in the palace, so his wife sought the counsel of Prime Minister Xiao He. Xiao He lured Han Xin into the palace, and had him executed on a charge of treason.

This story was summarized into the proverb "Success or failure, Xiao He is the man behind it," implying that the success or failure of situation is due to the same person.

---

* Gaixia is the name of a place in ancient China, 300 kilometers or so north of Hefei, capital of present-day Anhui Province.

成 由 勤 俭 败 由 奢

chéng yóu qín jiǎn bài yóu shē

Thrift leads to success, luxury results in failure

春秋时期，戎国国王派使者由余去见秦穆公。秦穆公听说由余是个贤士，就向他请教说："我常常听人谈论圣人治国之道，但没亲眼见过。请问先生，古代君主使国家兴盛和灭亡的原因是什么？"由余回答道："臣尝闻之矣，常以俭得之，以奢失之。"意思是说：我曾经听说勤俭使国家兴盛，奢侈使国家灭亡。

秦穆公听了，不高兴地说："我虚心向你请教兴盛之道，你怎么用'勤俭'二字来搪塞我呢？"由余说道："我听说，过去尧虽身为天下之主，却用瓦罐子吃饭、饮水，天下部落没有不服从他的。尧禅位于舜，舜开始讲究起来，用精雕细刻的木碗用餐，结果诸侯认为奢侈，国内有十三个部落不服从他的号令。舜禅位于禹，禹则更加讲究了，制作了各式各样精美的器皿供自己享用，奢侈就更加厉害了。结果国内有三十三个部落不听从号令。以后的君主越来越奢侈，而不服从号令的部落也越来越多。所以我才说勤俭是兴盛之道，奢侈是败亡之源。"这一番话说得秦穆公连连点头称是。

后来，唐代诗人李商隐根据这个故事，写了一首《咏史》诗。诗的前两句是："历览前贤国与家，成由勤俭破由奢。"

后来，"成由勤俭破由奢"演变为"成由勤俭败由奢"，并作为谚语流传下来，告诉人们，勤劳俭朴有助于事业的成功，贪图享受则会带来严重的恶果。

In the Spring and Autumn Period, You Yu was sent by the king of a kingdom named Rong as an envoy to visit Duke Mu Gong of the State of Qin. The duke said to You Yu: "I have often heard that sagacious men had their way to administer the states but I have never had a chance to see it. Could you tell me how ancient kings caused the rise and fall of their kingdoms?" You Yu answered: "Industry and frugality make a country prosperous while luxury and extravagance make a country perish." Hearing this, the duke said unhappily: "I sincerely consulted you about the way to prosperity. How come that you stall me off by talking about 'industry' and 'frugality'?" You Yu said: "Your Majesty, I am not stalling you off. I heard that the early monarch Yao ate and drank with clay vessels and therefore won the respect and obedience of every tribe under heaven. When Shun accepted the throne abdicated by Yao he was a fastidious man and used very fine wooden bowls for eating. Many dukes were disgruntled by his excessive lifestyle and 13 tribes began to disobey his orders. Later when Yu* assumed the throne abdicated by Shun he was even more particular in his tastes, having many exquisite and costly vessels made just for his own use. He really went overboard in his extravagance ways. As a result, 33 tribes refused to follow him. Since then, the dukes became increasingly extravagant as more and more tribes disobeyed them. That's why I say thrift and industry are the root of prosperity while luxury is the root of destruction." Duke Mu Gong nodded in agreement.

Based on this story the famous Tang Dynasty poet, Li Shangyin, wrote a poem which reads: Looking back to the emperors of the past ages, the thrifty ones administered the country well but the luxurious ones only ruined the state. This story gave rise to the proverb "thrift leads to success; luxury results in failure," meaning that industry and frugality are guarantees to success but indulging in a life of pleasure and covetousness will bring extremely grave consequences.

---

* Yu was a legendary monarch of ancient China, the successor of Shun, the reputed founder of Xia Dynasty (c. 21st-16th century B.C.).

死马当作活马医

sǐ mǎ dàng zuò huó mǎ yī

Treating a dead horse as if it were alive

西晋末年，河东有位很有成就的诗人郭璞，他不仅诗赋写得好，而且还见多识广，经常为人们释疑解难。

有一年，郭璞的家乡遭受战乱，他带着亲戚朋友数十家到江南去避乱。途中经过大官僚赵固将军的住所，郭璞前去拜访。不巧赵固的一匹骏马刚死，赵固正为此伤心，不愿见客。郭璞对守门人说："吾能活马。"（我能将此马医活）守门人很吃惊，赶快进去通报。赵固一听，急匆匆地跑出来对郭璞拱手说："您真能治活我的马吗？"郭璞说："是的。您立即叫上二三十个壮夫，带上长竹杆，往东行走三十里处，有一片茂密的树林。到了那里，便围着树林拍打。那时会得到一个活物，赶紧把它带回来，有了这个活物，马就得救了。"赵固按照这个吩咐去做，果然提回来一个长相像猴子的动物。这个动物见到死马，便伏到马的鼻子上不停地吹气。一会儿那马苏醒过来，再过一会儿，竟一声长鸣，翻身站了起来。赵固非常高兴，赶忙招呼手下人摆宴款待郭璞，并捧出黄金百两送给他。

根据这个故事，后人引申出"死马当作活马医"这个谚语，用以比喻明知无效，也要作最后努力，尽力挽救。

At the later stage of the Western Jin Dynasty, there was an accomplished poet named Guo Pu living near the eastern bank of the Yellow River. He was known not only for his literary works, but also for his wide range of knowledge and experience, so people would often consult him on tough problems.

One year, Guo Pu's hometown was torn by war. Bringing a number of relatives and friends with him, he evacuated to the south of the Yangtse River. As they passed the residence of a bureaucrat and general named Zhao Gu, they decided to go in for a visit. Unfortunately, Zhao refused to meet anyone at this time because he was mourning over the recent death of one of his horses. Guo told Zhao's gate-keeper that he could bring the horse back to life. The servant, astounded, immediately reported this to his master. Zhao rushed out and, after having paid obeisance to Guo, asked, "Can you really revive my horse?" "Yes, I can," Guo said. "You may ask 20 or 30 strong men to bring long bamboo poles and walk east for about 30 *li*, and they will see a thick wood there. They should surround the wood and beat the trees with the poles and a living creature will appear. They should bring this creature back without delay. Once you have this creature, your horse's life can be restored." Zhao did just as Guo said and, as expected, his men brought a monkey-like creature back to him. Upon seeing the dead horse, this creature jumped onto the body and kept blowing air into the horse's nose. After a while, the horse came to and woke up, and, soon afterward, the horse got back on its feet and stood up with a loud neigh. Zhao was overjoyed and wasted no time to prepare a banquet for Guo, and gave him a hundred taels of gold as token of gratitude.

120

This story later gave rise to the expression "treating a dead horse as alive." It means although one knows his effort will have no effect, he still tries his best to save the situation.

死诸葛走生仲达

sǐ zhū gě zǒu shēng zhòng dá

A dead Zhuge frightening off
a living Zhongda

诸葛亮是三国时著名的政治家。在他病危的时候，蜀军正与魏军对阵。诸葛亮知道自己将死，就把大将杨仪、姜维找来，嘱咐他俩："我本想竭力尽忠，夺取中原，想不到得了不治之症。我死之后，你们可如此如此。这样，司马懿必不敢来追。"说完不久，诸葛亮便闭上了眼睛。

　　杨仪、姜维遵照诸葛亮遗嘱，不敢举哀。入殓以后，暗传密令，让前军作后军，后军作前军，悄悄退去。当地老百姓见蜀军撤退，有的就跑去报告司马懿。司马懿半信半疑，就派人到五丈原一看，果然蜀军退尽，这才率兵追赶。眼看就要追上，忽听到前面山中喊声大振，锣鼓齐鸣，似有千军万马杀出。司马懿大吃一惊，只见山林里飘出一面大旗，上有一行大字："汉丞相武乡侯诸葛亮。"司马懿以为中了埋伏，急忙命令军队撤退。士兵们丢盔弃甲，争先逃命。杨仪、姜维并不追赶，而是率领大军向蜀国撤退。等到司马懿知道上了当，已经追不上了。

　　这事很快传到了老百姓中间，人们无不佩服诸葛亮用兵如神，死后还能降住司马懿，于是他们就用"死诸葛走生仲达（司马懿的字）。"（意思是：死后的诸葛亮吓跑了活着的司马懿）来表达他们的敬爱之情。

　　后来，人们用这一谚语比喻聪明有才干的人挫败了胆小或愚笨的人。

Zhuge Liang was a renowned politician of the Three Kingdoms Period. He was very ill when the Shu army under his command was in a crucial confrontation with the Wei troops. On his death bed, he summoned generals Yang Yi and Jiang Wei into his room for his final instruction. He said, "I have tried my best to help the emperor conquer Central China, showing my faith and loyalty. But I have caught a terminal disease now. After my death, this is what you should do. Do just as I tell you. In this way, Sima Yi will not dare to chase after you." With these words Zhuge Liang closed his eyes forever.

Yang Yi and Jiang Wei, followed Zhuge Liang's final instructions and did not disclose the news of his death. When Zhuge's remains were encoffined, the army received a secret order to make a clandestine retreat with the vanguard taking the position of the soldiers at the rear and vice versa. Sima Yi, also known as Zhongda, heard about this from some local residents who saw the retreat of the Shu army. Sima Yi, half-convinced, sent out scouts to the enemy's campsite. Seeing that the enemy had really retreated, Sima Yi led his troops to chase them down. When they came near the retreating enemy, they suddenly heard cries and the beating of drums and gongs from the hills before them, as if thousands of soldiers and horses had rushed out at them for a fight. In a state of shock, Sima Yi saw a large banner, with the characters "Zhuge Liang, Prime Minister of the Han and Marquis of Wuxiang," erected in the woods where the cries had came from. Sima Yi thought they were ambushed and urgently ordered his men to withdraw. His troops pulled out in panic, caring about nothing but their lives. Yang Yi and Jiang Wei did not pursue them and continued their own retreat. When Sima Yi learned that he was taken in, it was already too late to do anything about it.

When this story spread out, everybody admired Zhuge Liang's miraculous military skills, for he could beat Sima Yi even after he had died. The proverb "a dead Zhuge frightening off a living Zhongda," refers to an intelligent and capable man outwitting a coward or fool.

过 河 拆 桥

guò   hé   chāi   qiáo

Tearing down a bridge after crossing it

元朝末年，朝中有个大臣名叫彻里贴木儿的，很得元顺帝的信任。有一次，他看到当时靠科举考试选拔人才的办法有很多弊病，就上书给皇帝，提出废除科举制度，得到了顺帝的支持。可是朝中有一个名叫许有壬的参政却提出了反对意见。经过一番辨论，许有壬的意见不但没被接受，而且，顺帝还让他在宣读关于废除科举制度的诏书时，站在班首，以此造成他支持废除科举制度的假相。许有壬害怕遭到祸害，只好违心地服从。果然，许多不知内情的朝臣对他产生了误解。由于许有壬自己是通过科举考试而进入仕途的，因此很多官员讽刺他说："许参政可以说是过了河就拆桥的人呀！"许有壬听了，有口难辨，就称病不再上朝了。

后来，人们引用"过河拆桥"来比喻利用别人达到目的以后，就把别人一脚踢开。

Towards the end of the Yuan Dynasty, Emperor Shun Di had great faith and confidence in Cheri Temur, a senior minister in the royal court.

Once the minister submitted a report to the emperor proposing the abolishment of the imperial examination system for selecting men of talent, for he saw many faults in it. His proposal won the emperor's support. But Xu Youren, another senior official, was opposed to the idea. After a debate was held in the court, Xu's opinions were not accepted. Emperor Shun Di even ordered Xu to stand at the head of the task team when the imperial edict for the abolition was announced, so as to create the false impression that Xu was for the action. Afraid of imperial anger and consequent persecution should he refuse the arrangement, Xu had to obey against his own will. At the time, many court officials who were ignorant of the true political situation, misunderstood Xu, who himself entered the official career by way of the imperial examination system. One of them said sarcastically, "Xu Youren is a man who tears down a bridge after he crosses it." Xu found it hard to clear himself, feigned illness and left the court for good.

This proverb is now used to describe someone who gets rid of others after making use of them.

岁 寒 然 后 知 松 柏

suì hán rán hòu zhī sōng bǎi

Only in the coldest winter
do pine trees show their mettles

孔子十分喜欢他的学生子路。有一次他夸奖子路说:"穿着破旧的棉袍子和穿着貂裘的达官贵人一道站着,却能泰然自若,毫不感到难为情,恐怕只有子路能做到吧!"子路听了,自然很高兴,脸上不免露出几分得意的神色。孔子怕他骄傲自满,又随口念了两句诗勉励子路:"不忮(zhì)不求,何用不藏?"(不嫉妒,不贪求,怎么会不好呢?)子路听后,不住地吟诵这两句诗。孔子说:"仅仅念在嘴上还不行,还要经得住实践的考验,岁寒,然后知松柏之后凋也。"

后来,"岁寒然后知松柏"被人们当作谚语,比喻只有经过严峻的考验,才能看出一个人的品质。

Once Confucius praised his favorite student Zi Lu, saying, "Only Zi Lu can manage to stay composed when he is dressed in rags in the company of officials and nobles dressed in fur." Zi Lu naturally was happy to hear this remark and could not help but beam with pride. Confucius, fearing that he would become complacent, quoted a poem to encourage him: "How can things go bad with a man without envy and greed?" Zi Lu repeatedly recited the two lines. Confucius said: "It is not enough just to recite the lines; they must stand the test of real life. Only in the coldest winter does one understand that pine trees are the last to wither."

Later, "only in cold winter do pine trees reveal themselves" became an idiom expressing that one's true character can only be seen after one goes through a severe trial.

庆 父 不 去　鲁 难 未 已
qìng fù bú qù　lǔ nàn wèi yǐ

As long as Qing Fu is not removed, there is no end to the trouble of the State of Lu

　　春秋时候，鲁庄公有位庶兄名叫庆父。此人不仅凶残狠毒，而且野心勃勃，时刻想谋篡君位。庄公活着的时候，他慑于庄公的威势，不敢轻举妄动。等到庄公一死，便开始行凶作乱。他先派人刺了继位做国君的子般，立了年仅八岁的庄公的儿子开为国君，史称鲁闵公。

　　当时，齐国最为强盛，齐桓公做着诸侯的霸主。他得知鲁国动乱不定，便派大夫仲孙去探听消息。仲孙回来报告说："不去庆父，鲁难未已。"（意思是：不除掉庆父这个人，鲁国的祸难不会停止）。齐桓公问："怎么才能除掉他呢？"仲孙回答："庆父积怨太深，必会自取灭亡。"

　　果然不久，庆父又把闵公杀死。这激起了鲁国人的义愤，纷纷要求惩处他。庆父看形势不妙，只好逃到莒(jǔ)国（今山东莒县一带）去。庆父逃走后，齐桓公派人拥立了鲁僖公。僖公立即用重金贿赂莒国，要求将庆父送回鲁国处置。庆父听到这个消息，就上吊自杀了。

　　"庆父不去，鲁难未已"这条谚语比喻不把制造祸乱的人除掉，就别想安宁。

In the Spring and Autumn Period, Duke Zhuang Gong of the State of Lu, had a half brother, Qing Fu, who was not only cruel and sinister but also ambitious. His mind was set on usurping the throne. When Duke Zhuang Gong was still alive, Qing Fu, fearing his power and influence, dare not act rashly. As soon as the duke died, Qing Fu began to carry out his conspiracy. First, he had the duke's successor Zi Ban assassinated, and then he crowned the duke's son, the eight-year-old Kai, as the new monarch of Lu. In history, he is known as Duke Min of Lu.

At the time, the State of Qi was the most powerful of all the states, and Duke Huan Gong of Qi, naturally became the overlord. When he learned that the State of Lu was in a state of chaos, he sent Zhong Sun, an official, to make an investigation. Zhong Sun returned and reported, "As long as Qing Fu is not removed, there will be no end to the trouble of the State of Lu." Duke Huan asked Zhong Sun, "What must we do to get rid of him?" Zhong Sun said, "He has incurred so much resentment and hatred for such a long time that he is doomed in self-destruction."

As expected, Qing Fu murdered Duke Min soon afterwards, which caused widespread indignation among the Lu people who demanded for Qing Fu's punishment. Qing Fu, sensing the hostility in the air, ran off to the neighboring State of Ju. After Qing Fu took to his heels, Duke Huan Gong helped to install a new monarch for Lu, known later as Duke Xi Gong. Once in power, Duke Xi Gong immediately tried to bribe the State of Ju into extraditing Qing Fu. After hearing this news, Qing Fu committed suicide.

This saying means that peace comes only when the troublemaker is removed.

杀 鸡 焉 用 牛 刀?
shā   jī   yān   yòng   niú   dāo

Why use a butcher's knife to kill a chicken?

　　孔子有位学生名叫子游，在鲁国的武城（今山东费县附近）做县令。一次，孔子带着几个弟子到武城去。当他们来到子游家门前的时候，院内传来一阵弹琴、唱歌和读书的声音。孔子想，子游不错，居然能够在这小地方兴办了学校，心里十分高兴。见面行礼之后，孔子有心想试探一下子游，就笑着对他说："'杀鸡焉用牛刀，'治理这么个小地方，也用得着教育吗？"

　　子游听了回答说："过去我听老师您教导过我：做官的人经过礼乐教化，就会有仁爱之心，待人相敬相爱；平民百姓经过礼乐教化，也就懂得遵循政令。"

　　孔子听了，马上对旁边的几位学生说："你们听着，子游讲的话非常对。我刚才说的不过是开个玩笑罢了。"

　　后来，人们把"杀鸡焉用牛刀"用作谚语，比喻办小事，无须花费大力量。

Confucius had a student named Zi You, who served as county magistrate in Wucheng, a small town in the State of Lu. Once Confucius went to Wucheng accompanied by several students. As they arrived at Zi You's house, they heard the playing of musical instruments, singing, and reading from the yard. Seeing that Zi You could set up a school in such a small place as Wucheng, Confucius was very pleased for him. Having exchanged greetings with Zi You, Confucius wanted to test him and said smiling, "Why must you use a butcher's knife to kill a chicken? Do you really need to promote education in such a small town?"

Zi You answered, "You taught me that when officials become culturally enriched, they will foster a heart of benevolence and love and treat others with respect and love; when the common people receive an education, they will understand how to follow orders and be law-abiding citizens."

Confucius turned to the students standing next to him, saying, "Are you listening? What Zi You said is very instructive. I was only trying to crack a joke."

Later the phrase "Why use a butcher's knife to kill a chicken?" came to mean that to handle a small matter does not require major efforts.

尽 信 书 不 如 无 书

jìn xìn shū bù rú wú shū

Blindly believing the whole book
is worse than having no book

孟子是战国中期儒家的代表人物。他读书十分爱动脑筋，从不轻易相信前人记述。有一次，他读古代典籍《尚书》，看到有这样一段记载说，周武王讨伐商纣王，杀得血流成河，连大木棒都漂了起来。看到这一记述，孟子不禁哑然失笑。他把一些学生找来，对他们说："尽信《书》则不如无《书》。"学生们都感到奇怪，就询问为什么。孟子说："我刚才读《尚书·武成篇》，其中记载武王伐纣，血流漂杵的话。你们想想，以周武王这样极其仁爱的贤君，去讨伐商纣王那样最不仁爱的暴君，义师所至，百姓欢迎，又怎么会发生血流成河，连舂米的大木棒都被漂走的事呢？"学生们听了，这才恍然大悟，更加佩服自己的老师了。

谚语"尽信书，不如无书"便是出自这个故事。"书"本指《尚书》，用在此谚语中，则泛指书籍，用以说明盲目相信书本是不行的。

Mencius was representative of the Confucian school during the Warring States Period. When he read books, he was extremely analytical, never lightly accepting the records of his predecessors. Once he read in *The Book of Documents* that during a battle launched by King Wu of the Zhou Dynasty against King Zhou of the Shang Dynasty, so many people were killed that the spilled blood became a stream so torrential that even wooden trunks could float in it. Unable to stifle his laughter at this account, Mencius summoned some students and said to them: "Blindly believing the whole *Book* is even worse than having no *Book*." The students did not understand their teacher and asked him why. Mencius explained, "I just read the chapter on Wucheng in *The Book of Documents*, which records King Wu's expedition against King Zhou. In the war, the blood of the slain flowed like a stream, which could even float wooden trunks. Now think about this. Just imagine the benevolent and virtuous King Wu of Zhou attacking the least benevolent and most tyrannical King Zhou of Shang. How could his righteous army, which was welcomed everywhere by the common people, allow blood to be shed like a river, with rice-husking pestles floating in it?" The students saw the light and respected their teacher even more.

In the saying "blindly believing the whole book is even worse than having no book," the book originally referred to *The Book of Documents*, but it now can refer to books in general. The proverb means that it is not good to blindly believe what a book says.

远 水 不 救 近 火

yuǎn shuǐ bú jiù jìn huǒ

Distant water can't put out a fire nearby

在春秋时各诸侯国中，鲁国是个小国，常常遭受大诸侯国的欺侮。鲁穆公即位以后，想改变自己势单力薄的状况，便把几位公子分别送到晋、楚等大国去学习，借以结交大国，目的是在鲁国发生危难的时候，能得到这些大国的援助。鲁穆公送公子们去的国家离鲁国都很远，而同鲁国毗邻的齐国他却不愿派人去。大夫犁钽(chú)认为这样做很不妥，就劝谏鲁穆公说："假如鲁国有个小孩子掉到河里；有人说：'越国人很会游泳，还是派人到越国请人来救吧！'越国和鲁国相距几千里，这个小孩子能得救吗？"

接着犁钽又打了一个比方说："假如我们鲁国的宫殿失了火，有人说：'大海里水充足，派人到海里取水灭火吧！'海水虽然很多，但这火一定无法扑灭，这是因为'远水不救近火'啊！现在晋国与楚国虽然比较强大，可是离鲁国太远，只怕一旦形势危急，晋国和楚国救我们也来不及。因此，我认为还是加强同齐国的友好关系才对。"鲁穆公认为犁钽的建议有道理，就采纳了。

后来，人们用"远水不救近火"比喻所设想的办法，不能解决急待解决的问题。

During the Spring and Autumn Period, the tiny State of Lu was frequently bullied and harassed by stronger dukedoms. After Duke Mu Gong assumed the throne, he tried to alter the situation by sending his princes to large states like Jin and Chu for study. His purpose was to forge alliances with these states so that in case Lu was in danger they might come to its rescue. The states chosen were all far from Lu, and Duke Mu Gong was unwilling to send his princes to the neighboring state, Qi. Li Chu, a senior court official who had a different opinion, said to Duke Mu Gong, "If a kid fell into a river in our state, someone might say, 'people in the State of Yue are good at swimming. Why not ask them to come and rescue the kid?' But because the State of Yue is thousands of *li* away from Lu, how can the kid be saved in time?"

Then Li Chu drew another analogy, "If our palace caught fire, someone might say, 'There is enough water in the sea. Now let people fetch water from the sea to put out the fire.' Of course the sea is full of water, but the fire will not be quenched in time. This is because water from afar cannot put out a fire nearby. Although the states of Jin and Chu are powerful, they are far from Lu. In case of danger, it will be too late if we wait for their assistance. Therefore, I think it is right to strengthen our relationship with the State of Qi." Duke Mu Gong found Li Chu's suggestion reasonable and adopted it.

Now people use the proverb "distant water can't put out a fire nearby" to describe the failure of a decision to solve the problem at hand no matter how well-conceived it is.

近水楼台先得月

jìn shuǐ lóu tái xiān dé yuè

A waterside pavilion sees the moon first

北宋时期，有一位著名的政治家、文学家叫范仲淹。为官期间，他知人善任，爱才惜才，许多年轻人靠他的提携得以施展才干。范仲淹在杭州做知州时，把部下按照其才能的大小一一推荐做了官。只有一个叫苏麟的人，因出外巡查不在知州府内，被范仲淹一时忽略了，没有得到相应的提拔。为此，苏麟有些情绪，但又不好明说，就写了一首诗寄给范仲淹。诗中有这样两句："近水楼台先得月，向阳花木易为春。"诗的表面意思是：靠近河边的楼台亭阁，最先得到月光的照临；朝着太阳的花草树木，最容易得到春天的温暖而萌发。实际的含意是说：在您身边的人都得到了提拔，而我不在您身边就被您遗忘了。

　　范仲淹看了这首诗，禁不住笑起来，不但没有生气，还称赞诗写得好。于是就立即写了一封推荐信给朝廷。不久，苏麟也被提升担任更高一级的职务。

　　后来，"近水楼台先得月"被人们当作谚语使用，比喻因所处位置的近便，而优先获得利益或照顾。有时也用来讽刺利用职权攫取利益的可耻行为。

Fan Zhongyan was a famous politician and man of letters in the Northern Song Dynasty (960–1127). When he served as a government official, he helped to groom many talented young people for official careers, guiding and supporting them to give full play to their capabilities. When he was the governor of Hangzhou, many of his students were appointed to different court positions according to their respective talent with Fan's recommendation. But one of Fan's subordinates, Su Lin, was away on an inspection tour when Fan was making his recommendation list. His name was not on the list, and he failed to receive a promotion. Su became dejected and, finding it hard to speak his mind, he wrote a poem and sent it to Fan. Two lines of the poem read, "A waterside pavilion gets to see the moon first, just as the flowers and trees facing the sun herald spring first." The actual meaning of the lines is: all your followers have been promoted but I have been forgotten because I was not by your side.

After Fan read the poem, he could not help laughing. Instead of becoming angry, he praised the poem as a well-written piece. He immediately wrote a reference letter to the imperial court. Before long, Su was promoted to a position higher than his peers.

The proverb "A waterside pavilion sees the moon first" has been derived from this story, expressing that one enjoys greater privileges and benefits as a result of one's advantageous location or position. It may also be used sarcastically to criticize those who shamelessly utilize their power and position in search of personal gains.

近朱者赤　近墨者黑

jìn zhū zhě chì　jìn mò zhě hēi

What is near red becomes red;
what is near black becomes black

　　北宋著名文学家欧阳修不仅在文学上取得了卓越的成就，而且还为当时的文坛培养了一批人才。像苏洵、苏轼、苏辙、曾巩、王安石等文学家都出自他门下，因而他当时很受人们的尊敬。

　　欧阳修在颍（yǐng）州（今安徽省阜阳市）当知州的时候，有位名叫吕公著的年轻人在他手下当通判（帮助知州管理行政事务）。有一次，欧阳修的朋友范仲淹路过颍州，顺便拜访欧阳修。欧阳修热情招待，并请吕公著作陪叙话。谈话间，范仲俺对吕公著说："近朱者赤，近墨者黑。你在欧阳修身边做事，真是太好了。应当多向他请教作文写诗的技巧。"吕公著点头称是。后来，在欧阳修的言传身教下，吕公著的写作能力提高得很快。

　　后来，"近朱者赤，近墨者黑"这句话，被人们用来比喻接近好人可以使人变好，接近坏人可以使人变坏。

Ouyang Xiu, a famous writer of the Northern Song Dynasty, was known for his outstanding literacy achievements and his success in cultivating a number of literary talents. Writers like Su Xun, Su Shi, Su Zhe, Zeng Gong, and Wang Anshi were all his students, and this earned him even greater respect from the people.

When Ouyang served as governor of Yingzhou (present-day Fuyang, Anhui Province), a young man named Lu Gongzhu assisted him with local administrative affairs. One day, Fan Zhongyan, a friend of Ouyang's, stopped over at Yingzhou to pay a visit to Ouyang. Ouyang warmly greeted his friend and asked Lu to join them for a chat. During the talk, Fan said to Lu: "What is near red becomes red and what is near black becomes black. This is a good opportunity for you. Since you work closely with Ouyang, you should learn as much as you can from his poetry and prose skills." Lu nodded in agreement. Under Ouyang's personal instructions, Lu quickly improved his writing skills.

"What is near red becomes red; what is near black becomes black" refers to the impression that one who frequently associates with good people can become good and one having bad associates can become a bastard.

快 刀 斩 乱 麻
kuài   dāo   zhǎn   luàn   má

Cutting entangled jute with a sharp knife

南北朝时期，东魏孝静帝的丞相名叫高欢。高欢有好几个儿子。有一次，他想试试哪个儿子最聪明，就把他们都叫到面前，发给每人一把乱麻，要他们整理，并讲明看谁理得最快最好。

比赛开始后，别的孩子都赶快把乱麻一根根抽出来，然后再一根根理齐。这种方法速度很慢，一着急还会使麻结成疙瘩。所以孩子们都急得满头大汗。高欢的二儿子高洋与众不同。他找来一把快刀，把那些相互缠绕的乱麻几刀斩断，然后再加以整理，这样很快就理好了。

高欢见高洋这样做，很是惊奇，就问："你为何采用这个办法？"高洋应声答道："乱者须斩！"高欢听了十分高兴，认为这孩子将来必定大有作为。

后来，高洋果然夺取了东魏皇帝的王位，建立了北齐政权，自己做了北齐文宣皇帝。

根据这个故事，后人引申出"快刀斩乱麻"这个谚语，用以比喻采取果断措施，解决复杂问题。

Gao Huan, prime minister of the Eastern Wei Kingdom of the Southern and Northern Dynasties, wanted to know which of his sons was the cleverest. He summoned them and asked each of them to sort out a pile of entangled jute to see who could do it in the shortest time and in the best way.

When the competition began, the kids hurried to draw one thread after another from the pile and put them in order. This method was very slow, and the threads could easily become tangled again. The kids worked so anxiously as to perspire profusely. Only Gao's second son, Gao Yang, was an exception. He found a sharp knife, cut the entangled jute in half, and quickly put the threads in order.

Gao Huan was surprised to see Gao Yang's handling of the problem and asked, "Why do you do it this way?" "Anything entangled should be cut like this," replied Gao Yang. Gao Huan was pleased at this answer and convinced that this child would grow up to be a great man.

Later, Gao Yang seized the throne of the Eastern Wei Kingdom and set up the Northern Qi Kingdom with himself as the Emperor Wen Xuan in history.

This story gave rise to the proverb "cutting entangled jute with a sharp knife," which means taking resolute action to solve a complex problem.

闲 时 不 烧 香　急 来 抱 佛 脚

xián shí bù shāo xiāng　jí lái bào fó jiǎo

Embrace Buddha's feet when in dire need,
but burn no incense when things are normal

古时候，云南南部有一小国，官民都崇尚佛教，国内出家做和尚的人特别多。有的人犯罪当杀，为避免一死，便临时跑进寺庙，双手抱住佛像的脚，表示愿意出家为僧、痛改前非，国王因此赦免了他。这样的事发生多了，老百姓便编了条谚语说："闲时不烧香，急来抱佛脚。"后来，这个国家有位和尚到内地传经，于是把这条谚语也传了进来。

　　这条谚语被人们用来比喻平时不作准备，事到临头才慌忙应付。

In ancient times, there was a small state in south Yunnan in which officials and commoners alike believed in Buddhism, and many of them were tonsured and became monks. Some felons who had committed capital offences would try to avert the death penalty by running into a temple, embracing the feet of a statue of Buddha with both hands, and taking vows to become a monk and mend their old ways. The king, moved by this, pardoned them. When this happened again and again, people came up with the proverb: "Embrace Buddha's feet when in dire need, but burn no incense when nothing happens." Later, when a monk from this state traveled inland to disseminate Buddhism, this proverb spread to other parts of China.

This proverb describes people who, being ill-prepared for emergencies, are often thrown into a panic when the critical time comes.

识 时 务 者 为 俊 杰

shí   shí   wù   zhě   wéi   jùn   jé

He who knows the situation is a wise man

诸葛亮是三国时期著名的军事家、政治家。他在辅佐刘备之前，隐居在襄阳城西（今湖北襄阳西）二十里处的隆中，一边躬耕农田，一边读书，研究天下形势。他知识渊博，才能超群。他的好朋友司马徽、徐庶等人都认为他具有匡世之才，必定能做出一番事业。

当时，刘备势薄力单，被曹操打败，正依附在荆州刘表处。多次的失败教训，使刘备懂得了人才的重要。于是他四处打听，访求贤能之士。他听说当地有个叫司马徽的名士，很有声望，就亲自拜访求教。司马徽推辞说："儒生俗士，岂识时务？识时务者在乎俊杰，此间自有伏龙、凤雏。"刘备忙追问："请问伏龙、凤雏是谁？"司马徽却笑而不答。刘备再三苦苦哀求，司马徽才告诉他说："伏龙，是指诸葛亮；凤雏是指庞统。只要得到他们当中的一个，就可以安天下！"

刘备按照司马徽的指点，三顾茅庐，终于把诸葛亮请了出来。后来，在诸葛亮的帮助下，建立了蜀汉政权。

后来，"识时务者在乎俊杰"演变成"识时务者为俊杰"这句谚语，人们用以说明：只有能认清客观形势，并能顺乎形势发展的人，才是英雄豪杰。

Zhuge Liang was a noted strategist and statesman during the Three Kingdoms Period. Before serving as a consultant to Liu Bei, he lived a secluded life in Longzhong, 10 kilometers west of Xiangyang (present-day Xiangyang in Hubei Province), farming while reading books and studying current affairs. He was both knowledgeable and talented. In the eyes of his friends such as Sima Hui and Xu Shu, Zhuge was a man of extraordinary talent destined for greatness in the future.

At the time, Liu Bei had just been defeated by Cao Cao and was taking refuge in Jingzhou where his fellow clansman Liu Biao ruled as warlord. Repeated failures continually reminded him of the importance of having the support of capable people on his side. He began to look everywhere for talent. Upon learning about a local gentleman named Sima Hui who enjoyed considerable prestige among the masses, he went to seek his advice, but Sima declined, saying, "I'm only an ordinary countryfolk. How can I know the current political situation? Only those well-acquainted with the current situation are wise men. Men like the Sleeping Dragon and Young Phoenix fall into this category." When Liu Bei asked him who the Sleeping Dragon and the Young Phoenix were, Sima gave no answer but smiled. It was only at Liu's repeated request that he said, "The former refers to Zhuge Liang and the latter is none other than Pang Tong. You'll rule China if you can get either of them to help you."

Following Sima Hui's advice, Liu Bei did succeed in getting Zhuge Liang out of his secluded life after paying three visits to his thatched house. With Zhuge's help, Liu Bei established the Kingdom of Shu.

The saying "he who knows the situation is a wise man" became a proverb, meaning that only those who have a clear understanding of the objective situation and conform to the historical trend of the times are real heroes.

君 子 之 交 淡 如 水

jūn   zǐ   zhī   jiāo   dàn   rú   shuǐ

Friendship between gentlemen is like water

春秋时期，孔子到诸侯国推行自己的政治主张，却无人理会，孔子心灰意冷，便到山林中隐居。

有一天，他在深山中碰到了一位名叫桑雽（hù）的隐士，两人闲聊起来。孔子问桑雽说："我曾经多次遭受灾祸，亲戚朋友不但不援助我，反而更加疏远了，学生也离我而去，这是为什么呢？"

桑雽说："您没有听说这样一个故事吗？有个叫林回的人在逃亡中丢掉了价值千金的玉璧，却背负着别人家的婴儿逃跑。有人问他："你这样做为的是钱吗？可是小孩能值多少钱呢？为的是怕累赘吗？可是小孩子比玉璧累赘多了。你到底为的是什么呢？林回回答说：'你说的那是唯利是图的人的想法。凡是具有天性和正义感的人都会像我这样做的。'"

桑雽讲完了这个故事后接着说："那些唯利是图的人，一遇到穷困、灾祸侵害的时候，就会互相离弃；而正人君子却能一如既往地互相照应。这两种人的交往态度相差多远啊！君子之交淡如水，小人之交甘如醴；君子淡以亲，小人甘以绝。"意思是说：君子之间的交往，清淡得像水一样，小人之间的交往，甘美得像甜酒一样。但是，君子以清淡相交却相亲；小人以甘甜之利相交，一旦利尽，关系也就断绝了。

孔子听了十分佩服地说："我领教您的高见了！"说罢，告辞而去。

这是个寓言故事。后来，"君子之交淡如水"被人们广为引用，比喻正派人之间的交往不在乎金钱、财物，而应注重清廉、纯洁。

During the Spring and Autumn Period, Confucius went to the different ducal states to peddle his political views, but was cold-shouldered everywhere. Dejected, he began to live a secluded life in the mountain forest.

One day, in the forest, he met a hermit named Sang Hu. During the chat, Confucius asked: "I have met many setbacks. My relatives and friends do not help me, and day by day we grow further apart from each other. I've even been deserted by my disciples. Can you tell me the reason for this?"

Sang Hu answered: "Haven't you ever heard of this story? While fleeing into exile, a man named Lin Hui discarded a valuable piece of jade, yet carried a neighbor's baby on his back. Someone asked, 'Are you doing this for money? But how much can a baby be worth? Are you doing this to lighten your load? But a baby is even more burdensome than a piece of jade. What's your real motive?' Lin answered: 'What you have mentioned is the mentality of those who put profit before everything. But any righteous man with a sincere and kind nature would do as I do.'"

Sang Hu continued: "Those putting profit first will mutually abandon one another when encountering disasters or straitened circumstances; while gentlemen and righteous men will continue to look after one another under such conditions just like nothing has happened. What a stark contrast between these two kinds of attitudes! The relations between gentlemen is like water while that between petty men is like sweet wine. Water-like relations beget friendliness and profit-based friendship does not last long. Once the profit is gone, the relationship is broken off as well." Confucius commended him for his insight.

This fable gave rise to the well-known proverb "relations

between gentlemen is like water," meaning that relations between upright people entail no money or material wealth, but should only embrace honesty and purity.

君子无戏言

jūn zǐ wú xì yán

No joking from a gentleman

西周初年，周武王姬发死后，长子姬诵继承王位，即周成王。当时成王年幼，由周公姬旦辅助处理国政。这一年，唐国诸侯反叛朝廷，被周公派兵平息。消息传来的时候，成王正与他的弟弟叔虞玩耍。成王拾起一片梧桐叶，把它削制成象征着帝王权力的圭形状信物，送给叔虞，并开玩笑说："我以此封你为唐国国君。"那时，君王身边都有一位专门记载他们言行的史官。所以当成王说了这句话后，史官马上记录下来，并且请求成王选择吉日封立叔虞。成王说："吾与之戏耳。"史官说："天子无戏言，只要说出的话就要算数。"于是成王只好封叔虞为唐国国君。

后来，"天子无戏言"成为谚语，意思是君王不说不算数的话。此语又演变为"君子无戏言"，用以说明一个人许下的诺言，必须落实、兑现。

In the early Western Zhou Dynasty (c. 11th century-771 B.C.), Ji Song, the eldest son of Ji Fa, succeeded the throne to become King Cheng Wang after his father's death. As King Cheng Wang was quite young at that time, one of his clansmen Ji Dan was assigned to help him take care of state affairs. During Ji Song's reign, the duke of the State of Tang attempted to betray the court, but was quickly suppressed by Ji Dan's troops. When the news reached the capital, King Cheng Wang was playing with his younger brother Shu Yu in the garden. The king picked up a leaf from the Chinese parasol tree and made it into a *gui**-shaped object which symbolized the power of the king. He handed it to his brother and joked: "I hereby crown you as duke of the State of Tang." The official who recorded the words and activities of the king immediately took note of this saying and demanded the king to select a lucky day to confer the title on Shu Yu. The king refuted: "I'm only joking." The official replied: "'There should be no joking from a king.' Any words spoken by a king should be carried out." So King Cheng Wang could not but confer the title on Shu Yu.

Later on, "there should be no joking from an emperor" came to mean that an emperor should never say anything which he does not carry out later. By and by the saying changed into the proverb "there should be no joking from a gentleman," which means any promise a person makes should be made good and fulfilled.

---

* *Gui* is an elongated pointed tablet of jade held in the hands by ancient rulers on ceremonial occasions.

青出于蓝而胜于蓝

qīng chū yú lán ér shèng yú lán

Originated from indigo, blue is even bluer

战国末期，赵国有一位著名的唯物主义思想家，名叫荀况，又称荀卿、荀子。他著有《荀子》三十二篇，系统地反映了他的哲学和政治思想，对后世影响很大。"劝学"是《荀子》中的第一篇。作者在这篇文章中，比较全面地论述了学习的目的、意义、态度和方法，对人们具有深刻的启迪作用。文章中有这样一段话："学不可以已。青，取之于蓝，而青于蓝；冰，水为之，而寒于水。"意思是：学习是不应当停止和废弃的。青色染料是从蓝草中提炼出来的，但颜色比蓝草更深；冰是水凝结而成的，但比水更凉。

在这里，荀子以青与蓝，冰与水的关系作比喻，说明学生只要通过坚持不懈地刻苦学习，就能够有所提高，甚至可以超过他的老师，取得更大的成就。后来，这几句话演变为"青出于蓝而胜于蓝"这句谚语，用以比喻学生胜过先生，后人胜过前人。

Towards the end of the Warring States Period, there was a noted materialist in the State of Zhao named Xun Kuang, or Xun Qing, or Xun Zi. His 32 essays in the book *Xun Zi* systematically reflected his philosophical and political ideas, which exerted a great impact on future generations.

An Exhortation on Studying, the first essay in the book, presents a comprehensive discussion on the goal and significance of learning, as well as the proper attitude to and method for learning. It is truly a revelatory work. In this essay there are several sentences like these: "There should be no end to learning. Blue dye is derived from the indigo plant, but it is even bluer than the original plant. Ice is frozen water, but is colder than water."

Using the relationships between blue and indigo and between ice and water, Xun Zi tries to show that so long as one painstakingly applies himself to one's studies, one will surely improve himself and may even be able to surpass the achievements and successes of one's teacher. Later on, the sentence "originated from indigo, blue is even bluer" is used as a metaphor to a student who may surpass his teacher or the younger generation which may surpass the older generation.

玩 火 者 必 自 焚

wán huǒ zhě bì zì fén

Those playing with fire are sure to burn themselves

　　春秋时期，卫庄公有个儿子名叫州吁，从小受到宠爱，养成了骄奢蛮横的性格。庄公死后，太子完继位做了国君，即卫桓公。州吁秘密结纳党羽，于公元前719年聚众袭杀了卫桓公，自立为国君。州吁知道自己的所作所为很不得人心，为了转移国内人民的视线，缓和矛盾，他联合宋、陈、蔡等国向郑国发动了战争。

　　鲁国国君鲁隐公听到这件事后，就问大夫众仲说："州吁这次篡位会成功吗？"众仲回答说："我听说安定百姓应该用德行，没有听说借用武力的。州吁这个人残忍无道，是没有多少人亲近他的。再说，用兵如引火一样，不知节制和收敛，到头来会连自己也被烧死。

　　果然，不到一年，州吁就被卫国老臣石蜡设计杀死，落得个"玩火自焚"的下场。

　　人们用"玩火者必自焚"这句谚语比喻冒险干坏事的人，最终害的是自己。

During the Spring and Autumn Period, Zhou Yu was the pampered son of Duke Zhuang Gong of the State of Wei. He was notorious for his arrogance and willfulness. After his father's death, his brother, the crown prince Wan, succeeded the throne as Duke Huan Gong. Zhou Yu and the gang he banded together killed Wan in 719 B.C. and made himself the duke of Wei. Zhou Yu knew he did not have the support of the people; so, to divert domestic attention, he ganged up with the states of Song, Chen and Cai to launch a battle against the State of Zheng.

When Duke Yin Gong of the State of Lu heard the news, he asked the opinion of his chamberlain Zhong Zhong: "Do you think Zhou Yu will succeed in his usurpation of the throne?" Zhong Zhong replied: "I know that the people will be pacified only by high morality rather than military force. Because Zhou Yu is so cruel, very few are on his side. Furthermore, commanding a military force is like kindling a fire. If one does not know when to restrain or relent, he is sure to end up burning himself."

Sure enough, less than a year later, Zhou Yu was killed in a scheme plotted by Shi La, a senior official of Wei. He ended up burning himself by playing with fire.

Hence the proverb "those playing with fire are sure to burn themselves" is used to describe those who plot against others recklessly eventually end up harming themselves.

苛 政 猛 于 虎

kē　zhèng　měng　yú　hǔ

An oppressive government is fiercer than a tiger

孔子有一次带着他的学生路过泰山，远远听到哭泣声，走近一看，原来是一位中年妇女趴在一座新筑的坟头上伤心地痛哭。孔子站在车上倾听了一会，就让子路劝慰她。子路来到妇人面前，好不容易才劝住了她的哭泣。子路问："您这样悲哀，有什么伤心事？"妇女哽咽着说："从前老虎咬死了我的公公；前不久，老虎吞吃了我的丈夫；现在我的儿子也惨死于虎口之下。"这时孔子也走下车，听到妇人的话就问："那您为什么不离开这老虎出没的地方呢？"妇人说："这里虽然危险，但是没有苛捐杂税，没有残暴的官吏，所以我们才来这里的。"孔子长叹一声，对子路说："子路你记住，苛政猛于虎也。"

　　后来，"苛政猛于虎"作为谚语流传下来，人们引用它形容暴虐残酷的压榨，给人民带来深重的灾难。

Once, when Confucius and his disciples passed by Mount Tai in Shandong Province, they heard of someone wailing. Drawing near, they found the crying was coming from a middle-aged woman kneeling by a newly-built grave. Confucius asked his student Zi Lu to comfort the woman. After Zi Lu had soothed her wailing, he asked: "May I know what is the cause of your sadness?" Choked with sobs, she said: "My father-in-law was bitten to death by a tiger years ago. Not long ago, another tiger swallowed my husband. Now my son has died, again between the teeth of a tiger." Hearing this, Confucius stepped out of his chariot and asked: "Then why don't you leave the place hunted by so many tigers?" The woman answered: "Although it is dangerous here, it is faraway from exorbitant taxes and levies, and cruel officials. That is why my family moved here." Confucius sighed to Zi Lu: "Zi Lu, you should always remember that an oppressive government is fiercer than a tiger."

This proverb describes how a cruel oppressive government can bring untold suffering to the people.

物以类聚 人以群分

wù yǐ lèi jù rén yǐ qún fēn

Animals of the same breed flock together, and so do people of the same breath

　　战国时期，齐国朝内有个名叫淳于髡的大臣，为人正派，善于言辞。有一次，他听说齐宣王要招贤纳士，就在一天之内，推荐七名贤士给齐王。齐王感到奇怪，就对淳于髡说："雫你一天之内竟举荐七人，这贤士不也太多了吗？"

　　淳于髡笑了笑说："鸟儿总是同类的聚在一起，野兽也是同类的在一道行走。如果到沼泽地里去找柴胡、桔梗一类的药材，那一辈子也找不到一根；如果到皋黍山、梁父山北坡去找，那就多得用车子也拉不完了。一切事物都是同类相聚的。我淳于髡就是贤士类中的人，成天与贤士生活在一起，让我找贤士就如同让我到河里打水、用火石取火一样容易。我还要向大王推荐贤士，哪会只这七个呢？"

　　谚语"物以类聚，人以群分"就是来源于这个故事。现多用来比喻坏人之间臭味相投，互相勾结在一起。

During the Warring States Period, there was a minister named Chunyu Kun in the State of Qi who was upright and had the gift of the gab. When he heard that Duke Xuan Wang of the state desired to recruit men of virtue to serve the court, he immediately recommended seven men to the duke in a single day. The surprised duke asked Chunyu: "You've recommended seven men of virtue to me within one day, how could there be so many of them?"

Chunyu smiled: "Birds of a feather flock together; and beasts of the same kind walk together. You would hardly find any herbs like platycodon root or bupleurum root if you look for them in a marsh; but if you search for them on the northern Gaoshu or Liangfu Mountain, you'll find an abundance of them there. The same is true with fauna and flora. I, Chunyu Kun, am a man of virtue and so are my friends. So, it's as easy for me to look for them as to fetch water from a river or get fire from a flint. Someday I'll recommend even more of them to you."

The proverb "animals of the same breed flock together, and so do people of the same breath" derives its origin from the above-mentioned story. Nowadays, it is often used in a derogatory sense to describe the collaboration of bad elements.

周 瑜 打 黄 盖——
zhōu yú dǎ huáng gài
一个愿打一个愿挨
yí gè yuàn dǎ yí gè yuàn ái

Zhou Yu beats Huang Gai—
the former wants to beat somebody and
the latter is willing to be beaten

公元 208 年，曹操率领八十万大军进攻南方，企图一举消灭刘备和孙权，统一天下。吴主孙权委任青年将领周瑜为"大都督"，统帅三军，与刘备的人马组成联军，共同抗击曹操。

周瑜是一个有勇有谋的战将。他经过周密的考虑以后，决定采用"火攻"战术对付曹操。可是曹军防守严密，引火船只无法接近曹操水寨。这天晚上他独自苦苦思考，老将黄盖悄悄走进军帐，对他说："若要火攻，必须派一人诈降，而要使曹操相信诈降者，还须行'苦肉计'。为了吴国，我愿一试。"

第二天，周瑜将众将召集到军帐里，商讨长期抗敌的对策。话未说完，黄盖站出来说："依我看，早早投降，才是上策！"周瑜勃然大怒，说："谁敢说投降，就杀掉他！"说完命令左右将黄盖推出斩首示众。众将官苦苦哀告，周瑜才免黄盖一死，叫人剥了他的衣服，当众打了五十大棒。黄盖被打得皮开肉绽，鲜血淋漓，昏过去几次。

黄盖被人扶到军帐后，立即派心腹去曹营递了降书，诉说自己受辱挨打之事，并表示甘愿替曹操效命。 此时，曹操已从其他渠道得到黄盖遭受毒打的消息，因而对黄盖之言未曾怀疑。于是双方约定几天之后，黄盖驾船来降。

到了约定的那一天，黄盖押着二十只装满引火之物的大船，乘着东风，直奔曹营水寨。在离水寨很近的地方，一齐点火。火借风势，风助火威，霎时间，曹操的战船全部着火。这场大火把曹军的战船全部烧光，人马死伤无数，曹操本人也差点送了性命。

根据这个故事，后人引出"周瑜打黄盖－一个愿打，一个愿挨"这个谚语，用以比喻做某件事情，两厢情愿。

In 208, Cao Cao led a strong army consisting of 800,000 soldiers down south in an attempt to wipe out the forces of Liu Bei and Sun Quan and unify the country. Sun Quan, king of the Kingdom of Wu, appointed the young general Zhou Yu as commander of the joint forces after forming an alliance with Liu Bei.

Zhou Yu was both brave and resourceful. After careful consideration, he decided to launch an attack by means of fire. But fire-kindling boats could hardly close in on Cao Cao's heavily guarded headquarters.

One night when Zhou was cudgeling his brains on how to get near Cao's troops, veteran general Huang Gai walked into his military camp quietly and suggested: "If you want to launch a fire attack, you must first send someone to Cao to pretend surrender. To convince Cao of the feigned surrender, you must first employ the 'battered-body ruse.' I am willing to carry this out for the sake of our kingdom."

The next day, Zhou Yu summoned all the generals to his camp to arrange long-term resistance against the enemy. He had hardly ended his address when Huang Gai stepped out and said, "In my opinion, the best thing to do now is to surrender!" Enraged, Zhou shouted: "Whoever utters the word surrender will be killed!" So he ordered the executioner to put Huang to immediate death by decapitation. It was only after the repeated imploring of all the generals present that Huang was spared. He was stripped of his clothes and severely flogged 50 times until he was bruised and lacerated.

After Huang had been helped to back his camp, he immediately sent a trusted subordinate to Cao's camp, with a letter describing the humiliation Zhou Yu caused him and his appeal to switch allegiance to Cao Cao's side. By the time Cao heard the news of Huang being bullied, he was fully convinced of Huang's surrender and set the date for Huang's crossing over.

When the day came, Huang Gai led 20 big boats full of inflammable materials and sailed all the way to Cao's camps in the eastern wind. When the boats came near, Huang ordered the ignition. Cao's camps soon caught fire as the wind was blowing to Huang's favor. The fire destroyed all of Cao Cao's warships and took a heavy toll on Cao's generals and soldiers. Cao himself barely escaped with his life.

The story of Zhou Yu beating Huang Gai has been handed down as a proverb to become a metaphor of two parties consenting in doing something together.

狗咬吕洞宾 不识好人心

gǒu yǎo lǚ dòng bīn bù shí hǎo rén xīn

The dog bites Lü Dongbin for
it doesn't understand Lü's sympathy on it

传说天宫中住着一只神狗，名叫"哮天犬"。哮天犬本为二郎神所豢养，由于它帮助天兵天将捉拿齐天大圣孙悟空有功，被玉皇大帝看中，把它留下来，看守天宫大门。

　　这哮天犬跟随二郎神一向自由自在，后来进了天宫，受到天条禁令的约束，很不习惯，时间一长，不免做出一些出格的事情。诸如咬伤月里嫦娥的玉兔，打碎南海观音的玉瓶，踩死寿星的灵芝仙草等等。于是玉帝决定除掉它，派八仙去执行。

　　哮天犬自知闯了祸，早已逃之夭夭。八仙找遍了天庭地界，最后才在一处偏僻的山坳里发现它。八仙赶忙布下阵势，逐渐缩小包围圈。哮天犬看八仙从四面围了过来，知道末日到了，浑身缩作一团，颤抖不止。吕洞宾见此情景，不免起了恻隐之心，想悄悄放走它。此时哮天犬在想：反正横竖是死，不如拼他一场，或许还能拣条性命哩。于是，它一跃而起，径直奔了过来。吕洞宾见哮天犬奔到自己跟前，赶忙侧身抽步，准备放它过去。谁知哮天犬只想拼命，没有理会吕洞宾的用心。它对准吕洞宾的腿肚子狠狠咬下一口，撕下一块肉来，痛得吕洞宾眼泪直淌，瘫坐在地上，叫苦不迭。等到那七位大仙赶到时，那狗早已逃得无影无踪。吕洞宾不禁仰天叹息："以怨抱恩，好人难做啊！"七位大仙听了这话，顿时明白了一切，对他嘲讽说："这才是狗咬吕洞宾，不识好人心。"

　　后来，"狗咬吕洞宾，不识好人心"被人们当作谚语使用。比喻一片好心，却未得到好报。

Legend has it that there was a celestial dog named Xiao Tian living in the heavenly palace. It was originally kept by the celestial Er Lang. Because it had helped celestial troops in catching Monkey Sun Wukong, the Jade Emperor assigned it the honorable job of guarding the door of the heavenly palace.

Xiao Tian, accustomed to the leisurely and carefree days he had spent with Er Lang, found it hard to adjust himself to the discipline in the heavenly palace. After being there for a while, it was inevitable that the dog would overstep its place, such as biting the white rabbit kept by Chang Er in the moon palace, breaking the jade vase of the Goddess of Mercy, trampling to death the magic fungus nurtured by the God of Longevity, etc. So the Jade Emperor ordered the Eight Immortals to put the dog to death.

Knowing that it was in big trouble, the dog fled away before the Eight Immortals could reach it. After searching for a long time, the immortals finally found it at a deserted corner of a col. They immediately formed a circle and gradually closed in on the dog. Knowing that his days were numbered, Xiao Tian huddled himself up and trembled incessantly. Seeing it in such a dilemma, Lü Dongbin, one of the immortals, took pity on it and wanted to let the dog get away quietly. The dog thought: "Since I'm going to die, I might as well go out fighting. This may save my life." It then leapt up and pounced upon Lü. When Lü saw this, he stepped aside to let the dog pass. But since the dog was so set on fighting for its life, it paid no attention to Lü's sympathy. It jumped onto Lü and bit the immortal hard on his calf. The bite was so harsh that it sent Lü collapsing to the ground. When the other seven immortals came to help, the dog was nowhere to be found. Lü Dongbin heaved a deep sigh: "My goodness has been repaid with evil. It is really hard to be a good person!" The others, having realized what had happened, sneered: "This is the real case of a dog biting Lü Dongbin for it doesn't understand Lü's sympathy for it."

Since then, this proverb has often been used figuratively to describe requiting kindness with evil.

重赏之下 必有勇夫

zhòng shǎng zhī xià bì yǒu yǒng fū

A brave man is sure to step out
if you offer a high reward

唐朝时候，有位姓崔的相国在河中府（今山西永济县）境内建造了一座寺庙，名叫普救寺。崔相国死后，崔夫人带着女儿崔莺莺将灵柩停放在普救寺内，准备待崔夫人的侄儿、莺莺的未婚夫郑恒来后，一同回家下葬。

不料，距普救寺不远处有一伙贼兵，他们的首领名叫孙飞虎。他打听到崔相国之女是倾国倾城的绝世美人，顿生歹意，命令五千士兵，连夜将普救寺包围起来；扬言三日内交出崔莺莺与他成亲，否则就烧毁庙堂，杀尽僧侣。普救寺长老赶忙找到崔夫人母女商量。莺莺说道："现可询问两廊僧人，有谁能够退去贼兵，我便嫁与他为妻。"夫人无奈，只得同意。长老在法堂上将莺莺的话说了一遍。话音刚落，一位借宿在寺中的秀才张生答道："我有退兵之计，何不问我？重赏之下，必有勇夫；赏罚分明，其计必成。"夫人说："你退得贼兵，我聘你为婿。"张生说："一言为定，请夫人静候佳音。"

原来，张生有一朋友，姓杜名确，统兵十万，镇守在离普救寺四、五十里远的蒲关。当下，张生写了一封信，央求长老派了一名会武功的和尚，冲出重围，把书信送给了杜确。杜将军立即挥师来救，解除了贼兵的包围。

"重赏之下，必有勇夫"后来作为谚语流传下来，被人们用以说明奖赏优厚，必定会有自告奋勇者出来效力。

A prime minister named Cui had the Pujiu Temple built in Hezhong (present-day Yongji County, Shanxi Province) during the Tang Dynasty. After Cui passed away, his coffin was placed in the temple, with Madame Cui and her daughter Yingying watching over. They were waiting for the arrival of Madame Cui's nephew Zheng Heng, Yingying's fiance, so that together they could escort the coffin to their homeland for entombment.

Unbeknownst to them, there was a gang of bandits near the temple whose leader was Sun Feihu. Hearing that Cui Yingying was a woman of rare beauty, he ordered five thousand of his followers to encircle the temple, attempting to capture Yingying and take her back to be his wife. Sun threatened that if Yingying did not give herself up within three days he would burn down the temple and kill all the monks. The abbot of the temple consulted with Madame Cui and Yingying. The girl said: "Whoever in the temple has the resource to drive Sun's troops away, I'll marry him." Madame Cui could not but agree to the plan. When the abbot announced Yingying's offer, Zhang Sheng, a scholar who had put up for several nights in the temple, stepped out: "I have a plan to repulse the enemy. Why not ask me? A brave man is sure to step out if you offer a high reward." Madame Cui agreed: "If you can repulse the bandits, I'll let you marry my daughter." Zhang Sheng answered: "OK, then it is agreed. Madame, now you can just sit back and wait for the good news."

As the story goes: Zhang Sheng had a friend, Du Que, who was in command of a hundred thousand soldiers stationed in Puguan, only some 20 kilometers away from the temple. Zhang wrote a letter, and a monk who was quite good in *gongfu* was sent to break the encirclement and deliver the letter to Du. Receiving the letter, Du came to their rescue at once, and the bandits were repulsed.

"A brave man is sure to step out if you offer a good reward" was passed down as a proverb to describe the following situation: If the reward is handsome enough, volunteers are sure to come out to help.

食之无味 弃之可惜

shí zhī wú wèi　qì zhī kě xī

Hardly worth eating but not bad enough to throw away

公元 219 年，驻守在汉中的魏国大将夏侯渊在与刘备交战时，战败被杀，汉中失守。魏军统帅曹操深知汉中地理位置之重要，便亲自率领大军来攻打。刘备据险固守，使魏军无法取胜。双方相持了几个月，魏军人马困顿不堪，粮草也渐渐接济不上。对此，曹操深为忧虑，他想撤军，又怕失了面子，一时拿不定主意。

一天晚上，曹操又为战事犯愁，这时侍从送上一碗鸡汤。曹操喝着鸡汤，咀嚼着鸡肋，不禁有所感触。就在这时，值日官夏侯渊来问夜里的口令，曹操随口说："鸡肋。"

夏侯渊将口令传达给各军营。军官们都感到"鸡肋"这个口令实在有趣，并不觉得其中还有什么含意，只有主薄杨修听后低头沉思片刻，很快明白了曹操的用意，于是马上吩咐随从说："我们就要班师回京了，你们赶快整理行装，准备动身。"将领们都知道杨修是个十分机警聪明的人，都来向他请教。扬修说："夫鸡肋，弃之如可惜，食之无所得，以比汉中，知王欲还也。"这话的意思是：鸡肋这东西，把它丢掉可惜，吃它又没有什么肉。拿它来比喻我们在汉中作战十分贴切：放弃吧不甘心，攻打又攻打不下来；权衡利弊，看来只得放弃了。所以我知道魏王（曹操）要回去了。

果然第二天曹操下令收拾行装，立即从汉中撤军。

　　"食之无味，弃之可惜"这句谚语就是从这个故事得出的，用以比喻对某件事想放弃，又有些舍不得；不放弃，又没有什么意义。

In 219, Liu Bei defeated and killed Xiahou Yuan, a Wei general guarding Hanzhong, and seized the city. Knowing the strategic importance of Hanzhong, Cao Cao, the commander of the Wei troops, came himself to take back the place. But he could not succeed as Liu's troops were tenaciously entrenched against the onslaught. The two parties were locked in a stalemate for several months. Wei's troops were dog-tired, and faced logistic problems. Cao Cao was worried. He wanted to withdraw, but was afraid of losing face. He was in a dilemma.

One night, when Cao was pondering hard on the military situation in his camp, an attendant brought in a bowl of chicken broth for a night snack. While he was sipping the broth and chewing on the chicken rib, something suddenly dawned on him. By the time, the official on duty, Xiahou Dun, came into the camp asking for the password for the night. Cao answered at random: "chicken rib."

When the password was circulated around, all the officers and ranks-and-files felt that this password was very funny, but no one was aware of the significance of the word. Only the secretary-general Yang Xiu knew Cao's intention after pondering over the password for a while. He told his assistant: "We are soon pulling back to the capital. You'd better hurry up with your packing." Knowing Yang Xiu was sharp-witted and resourceful, all the officers came over for his advice. Yang said: "A chicken rib is like something you cannot bear to throw away, but it's also hardly worth eating since it doesn't contain much meat. It is an apt metaphor for the military situation in Hanzhong. We don't like the idea of abandoning Hanzhong, but we can't get it back either. Considering the losses and benefits, the best way is to abandon the city. So I know our commander is thinking of retreating."

Sure enough, the next day Cao Cao issued the order to pack up and withdraw from Hanzhong.

The proverb "hardly worth eating but not bad enough to throw away" is derived from the above-mentioned story, meaning that it is a pity if one throws something away, yet it serves no purpose to hold onto it either.

独 行 不 愧 影 独 寝 不 愧 衾

dú　xíng　bú　kùi　yǐng　dú　qǐn　bú　kùi　qīn

Don't feel ashamed while walking alone with one's shadow or facing one's quilt alone at night

南宋时期,有位著名的学者名叫蔡元定。他天资聪颖,八岁就能写诗,在父母的指点下,他勤奋好学,博览群书,学业大有长进。当时著名理学家朱熹在世,蔡元定慕名前往拜师求教。朱熹视他为老学友,让他和自己同宿一室,整日切磋学问,常常谈到深夜。

当时,朝廷宗室、丞相赵汝愚和外戚韩侂胄(zhòu)为争权而互相倾轧。结果,赵汝愚被罢了官,韩侂胄接替做了丞相。赵汝愚是朱熹的好友,曾推荐过朱熹为官。因而韩氏当政后,为了清除政敌,便罗织罪名陷害打击朱熹及其弟子亲朋。蔡元定听到要抓捕他的消息后,赶紧辞别朱熹,与儿子一道逃到三千里以外的南方隐居。当地远近学子听说蔡元定到来,都纷纷前来求学。蔡元定并不拒绝,每天聚众讲学,传授知识,一时间在当地影响很大。关心他的亲友深感不安,担心一旦让朝廷发现会对他下毒手,就劝他闭门谢客,遣散门徒。可是蔡元定却说:"他们是来求学的,我怎好拒绝呢?如果有灾祸,就是闭门不出也是躲避不掉的。"他还再三叮嘱儿子说:"独行不愧影,独寝不愧衾。"意思是:一个人独自行走,面对影子要不感到惭愧;独自睡眠,面对被子要不感到惭愧。

"独行不愧影，独寝不愧衾"后来作为谚语流传下来。这句谚语说明，为人处事，任何时候都要做到问心无愧。

During the Southern Song Dynasty (1127–1279), there was a noted scholar named Cai Yuanding. Endowed with extraordinary intelligence, he could write poems at the age of eight. Under the guidance of his parents, he studied diligently and read profusely. Thus he became a man of great learning. At this time, the well-known neo-Confucianist Zhu Xi was still alive. So Cai went over to Zhu's place and asked to be his student. Zhu accepted Cai as an old companion. Living in one room, they exchanged experiences and studied together during the day, and often had academic discussions late into the night.

At this time, Prime Minister Zhao Ruyu, one of the emperor's clansmen, and Han Tuozhou, one of the queen's relatives, vied with each other for political power. The final result was: Zhao was dismissed from office and Han took the position as prime minister. Zhao had once recommended his good friend Zhu Xi to serve in the court. So when Han came to power, in order to eliminate his political opponents, he cooked up charges against Zhu Xi as well as the latter's disciples, relatives and friends. When Cai heard of the news, he immediately said goodbye to Zhu and fled with his son to a place three thousand *li* away in the south. When local scholars heard of Cai's arrival, they came over one after another to become his disciples. Cai never refused any one of them. Instead, he held academic forums every day to pass on his knowledge. Gradually Cai became very influential in the local academic circles. Concerned with Cai's safety his relatives and friends advised him to disband his forums for fear that he might get caught. Cai disagreed. He said, "They come over to me for studying. How can I refuse them? If there is disaster, I wouldn't be able to escape it even if I stayed behind closed doors." He told his son time and again: "One should not feel ashamed while walking alone with one's shadow, just as one should not feel ashamed facing one's quilt when sleeping alone at night."

Cai's admonishment to his son is used today as a proverb meaning one should always have a clear conscience when dealing with people or situations.

恻 隐 之 心　人 皆 有 之

cè yǐn zhī xīn　rén jiē yǒu zhī

Sympathy is common nature for men

孟子的学生公都子,对人的本性善良与否弄不明白,便向孟子请教。

孟子回答说:"要说人的本性,都是向善的,就是我所说的'人性本善'。比如:恻隐之心,人皆有之。(意思是:怜悯他人的心,人人都有)。这种美德,不是由外面虚饰而成的,而是人的本身就具有的,只不过没有自觉地意识到罢了。为什么有的人的德行比别人相差甚远,原因就是因为他们不能充分发挥自己天生的美德啊!"

公都子听了这番话,信服地点了点头。

孟子所说的"恻隐之心,人皆有之"后来作为谚语流传下来,被人们经常用来说明对别人的不幸表示同情怜悯的心情,人人都有。

Gong Duzi, a disciple of Mencius, was puzzled whether man was born innocent and good. So he went to his teacher for an answer.

Mencius answered: "Human nature tends towards the good. For example, I believe sympathy is common to all men. This virtue cannot be construed as some kind of outward decoration, rather it is inherent in human nature, though many have not become conscious to that fact. The reason why some people are less virtuous than others is that they cannot give full play to their inborn virtue."

Convinced, Gong Duzi nodded in agreement.

This saying by Mencius is often used nowadays to mean that everyone has sympathy and compassion for others' misfortunes.

养 兵 千 日　用 兵 一 时

yǎng bīng qiān rì　yòng bīng yì shí

Training an army for a thousand days
to be used for just one hour

南北朝时期，文臣中有个名叫陈暄的人。此人颇有几分文才，作诗、写文章都很出色，只是行为放荡、举止轻浮。他最大的嗜好是饮酒，一天到晚喝得醉醺醺的，有时醉得跌下马来，有时醉卧在街道上。陈暄的侄子陈秀对此非常反感，但作为晚辈不好直接批评劝说，就写信给陈暄的好友何胥，让他出面劝陈暄不要酗酒。

不料，陈暄非但不听何胥的话，还写信给陈秀，为自己的行为辩解。他在信中列举了历史上有不少名人都爱饮酒的例子，说明饮酒有得有失。他说："我常把酒比作水，它可以渡舟，也可以覆舟。有人这样说：'酒犹兵也，兵可千日而不用，不可一日而不备。酒可千日而不饮，不可一饮而不醉。'"

后来"兵可千日而不用，不可一日而不备"两句话演变成"养兵千日，用兵一时"这句谚语，用以比喻平时做好准备，以便在必要时使用。

190

Chen Xuan, an official in the Southern and Northern Dynasties, was a talent in writing poems and essays. But his only flaw was his wanton and frivolous demeanor and his biggest hobby was drinking. He was often drunk from morning till night. In drunkenness, he often fell from his horse, or slept in the street. Chen Xiu, his nephew, was very much against Chen Xuan's behavior. But since he was the younger generation, he could not criticize his uncle directly. So he wrote to his uncle's good friend He Xu, asking the latter to admonish Chen Xuan not to indulge in excessive drinking.

Contrary to Chen Xiu's expectation, instead of listening to He Xu's admonishment, Chen Xuan wrote back to his nephew justifying his drunken behavior. In the letter, he listed many historical celebrities who loved to drink, just to show the merits and benefits of drinking. He wrote: "I often compare wine with water. Water can carry a boat, but it can also capsize a boat. Someone has said: 'Wine is like army soldiers. A country may not deploy its army in a thousand days, but it should maintain an army at all times. One may not drink wine for a thousand days, but once he drinks he should not stop until he is drunk.'"

Later on, the saying "Training an army for a thousand days to be used for just one hour" is used to mean one should normally stay prepared for the future.

前 车 已 覆 后 车 当 鉴

qián chē yǐ fù hòu chē dāng jiàn

An overturned chariot ahead should serve
as warning to those behind

汉文帝刘桓在位时期,朝内有位年轻的官员名叫贾谊。贾谊为人刚正,很有政治远见,曾多次上书汉文帝,直言陈述国家政事,受到文帝的赏识。

有一次,他在汉文帝的《陈政事疏》中,引夏、商、周三代统治数百年,而秦朝二世而亡的例证,劝汉文帝吸取历史教训。他说:"鄙语曰:'前车覆,后车戒。'意思是:前面的车翻了,后面的车子应当戒备。 秦朝之所以很快灭亡,其原因是显而易见的。 然而后人如果不引以为戒,那就要同秦朝一样,又将倾覆灭亡了。 因此,我们一定要深刻总结历史经验教训。 采取有力措施,防患于未然,这样才能使国家长治久安。"接着,贾谊列出了一系列建议。汉文帝认为贾谊的分析和建议很有道理,备加赞赏。 于是就提升他的官位,拜他为太子太傅(辅导太子的官)。贾谊也更加忠心耿耿,不断上书针砭时弊,向汉文帝提了许多重要建议。

"前车已覆,后车当戒"后来演变为"前车已覆,后车当鉴"并作为谚语流传卜米,比喻应当接受前人失败的教训,不要再重蹈覆车之辙。

During the reign of Emperor Wen Di of the Han Dynasty, there was a young official named Jia Yi. Jia was upright, and also a man of incredible political foresight. He spoke frankly on state affairs in his many appeals to the emperor, and his advice earned him praise from the emperor.

In his *Memoir on Government Policy*, he advised the emperor to draw lessons from history. He pointed out that the Xia, Shang and Zhou dynasties had lasted for several hundred years respectively while Qin Dynasty only ruled for two generations. He wrote: "An overturned chariot that lies on the road ahead should serve as a warning to those behind. The reason for the downfall of the Qin Dynasty is obvious. But if no lesson is drawn, every reign will be just as short-lived as the Qin Dynasty. Therefore, we should sum up the historical experiences and draw lessons from them so that we can take preventive measures against any possibility of future disasters. Only thus can a state have lasting political stability." Then Jia made a list of suggestions. The emperor was so impressed that he made Jia the tutor of the crown prince. In return Jia showed even more loyalty in submitting memoirs in criticizing or making suggestions on current affairs.

"The overturned chariot ahead should serve as a warning to those behind" has been passed down as a proverb to admonish the later generations to draw lessons from the failure of their predecessors so that they may not repeat those errors.

既 得 陇 复 望 蜀

jì　dé　lǒng　fù　wàng　shǔ

Covet Shu after capturing Long

东汉光武帝刘秀手下有一员大将名叫岑彭。他作战骁勇，智谋过人，为朝廷打了很多胜仗，因此深得皇帝的器重和信任。

公元 32 年，岑彭跟随刘秀攻打不肯归顺的隗(kuí)嚣。几次交战之后，隗嚣丢兵弃甲，败逃到西域(今甘肃天水县南，属陇地)。这时候，占据蜀地的公孙述派大将李育率兵援救隗嚣。李育将大军开拔到上邽(guī)(今甘肃天水市)驻守。正当刘秀准备挥师进军的时候，后方发生叛乱。刘秀只好留下岑彭攻打西域和上邽，自己赶回去处理叛乱事件。回师途中，刘秀写了一封信给岑彭，提出下一步的行动计划。信中这样写道："两域若下，便可将兵南击蜀虏。人苦不足，既得陇(今甘肃东部)，复望蜀(今四川中西部)。每一发兵，头须为白。"意思是：如果打下西域和上邽，你们可以立即引兵南下攻打蜀地。人受苦受累，都是因为总不知满足；像我，既然得到陇地，却又想着获取蜀地。每次用兵，我的头发和胡须都要白一些的。

光武帝走后，岑彭采用了引水灌城的战术攻打西域，可是水深不到一丈时，救兵赶到，把隗嚣救走了。岑彭见军中粮食就要吃光，只好罢休，领兵回去了。

"既得陇，复望蜀"后来作为谚语流传下来，用以比喻得了这个，又想那个，不知满足。多用作贬义。

Cen Peng, a general under the reign of Liu Xiu, Emperor Guang Wu of the Eastern Han Dynasty, was a courageous fighter and brilliant strategist. Because he fought many successful battles for the state, the emperor held him in esteem. In 32, Cen Peng followed Liu Xiu in fighting Kui Xiao who refused to pledge allegiance to the Han Dynasty. After several battles, Kui Xiao was defeated and withdrew to Xiyu (south of present-day Tianshui in Gansu Province, called Long in ancient times). Gongsun Shu, who occupied the Shu area (central and western parts of present-day Sichuan Province), sent his general Li Yu to help Kui Xiao. Li stationed his troops in Shanggui (present-day Tianshui in Gansu Province). Just as Liu Xiu was preparing to march south, his home turf was in trouble. He had no choice but to leave Cen Peng to attack Xiyu and Shanggui and went back himself to deal with the rebellion at home. On his way back, he wrote a letter to Cen, putting forward his next plan of action. He wrote: "If you gain Xiyu and Shanggui, you may immediately march south to attack the Shu area. People suffer because of insatiability, and I'm one of them. Once I gain Long (present-day eastern part of Gansu Province) I set my eyes on Shu. Every time I employ the army for a battle, both my hair and beard turn a bit whiter."

After Liu Xiu's departure, Cen Peng used a flooding strategy to attack Xiyu. But before the flood waters got too deep, reinforcements arrived and rescued Kui Xiao. As there was insufficient grain to make it through the battle, Cen could not help but retreat.

This story gave rise to the proverb "covet Shu after capturing Long," which is often used today in a derogatory way to describe people having insatiable desires.

桃 李 不 言 下 自 成 蹊

táo   lǐ   bù   yán   xià   zì   chéng   xī

The peach and the plum do not speak, yet a path is worn beneath them

　　李广是西汉时期著名的将领。 他精于骑射，且作战勇敢机智，很令匈奴人敬畏。李广对待部下亦体贴爱护。行军打仗中，有时粮断水绝，他总是把水和食物让给士兵们。每次得到朝廷赏赐，他都拿来分给部下。 因此，李广深受士兵的爱戴，士兵都愿为他冲锋陷阵、拼死效力。 但这样一位受人尊敬的将领，一生却屡遭打击，晚年还落个悲惨的结局。

　　在李广六十多岁时，汉武帝任命他为前锋，随大将军卫青出击匈奴，可是卫青却不让他充当前锋，而让他领兵绕远路走东道。这分明是轻视他。李广争辩无效，只得从命。结果中途迷路，没能按时到达。卫青派人责怪李广及他的部下贻误战机。李广对来人说："我的部下将领无罪，责任在我一人，由我承担好了。"等来人走后，李广悲愤地对部下说："我自从入军以来，身经百战。 这次出击，本想先行与匈奴交战，没想到大将军把我的队伍调开，让我走那条迂回遥远的路径，以致迷路。 我现在已六十多岁，难道能等着受审治罪吗？"说完拔剑自刎而死。全军上下听到这一噩耗，个个失声痛哭，远近老百姓也都为之伤感流泪。

　　西汉史学家、文学家司马迁在《史记》中以深为同情的笔触，记述了李广一生的遭遇。最后他写下这样一段赞颂的话"余睹李将军悛悛如鄙人，口不能道辞。及死之日，天下知与不知，皆为尽哀，彼其忠实心诚信于士大夫也！谚曰：'桃李不言，下自成蹊。'此言虽小，可以喻大也。"这段话的意思是：我见过李广将军，他为人诚恳淳朴，就像个乡下人，也不善于讲话。但是他死的时候，天下了解与不了解他的人，都为他的死而难过，可见他忠实心诚的操行远远胜过了能说会道的士大夫！俗话说："桃树、李树凭着自己美丽的花、甜美的果，不向人们打招呼，人们也会自动前来，以致树下踩出了一条路。"这话虽然简短，却很说明大道理啊！

谚语"桃李不言，下自成蹊"最早见于这个故事中。比喻一个人只要真诚实干，必定会赢得人们的称赞。

Li Guang was a noted general during the Western Han Dynasty (206 B.C.-24 A.D.). He was good at horseback shooting, and was brave and resourceful in fighting against the Huns, an ancient nationality in China, thus rousing awe in the enemy. Li also loved and showed consideration for the troops under his command. If the supply grain or water was running short, he would give what was left to his subordinates. Every time he gained a reward from the court, he would divide it among his troops. As a result, Li Guang won the love and esteem of his subordinates who were all willing to lay down their lives for him in fighting the enemy. Yet such an esteemed general often met with setbacks in his political life and had a tragic ending.

When Li was in his sixties, the emperor appointed him as the vanguard general to accompany Wei Qing, the commander-in-chief in his attack on the Huns. Instead of sending Li as a vanguard, Wei, out of contempt, asked him to lead the troops in a roundabout march from the east side. After arguing with Wei to no avail, Li Guang could do nothing but obey. Because Li lost his way, he did not arrive on time. Wei sent one of his men to Li to criticize his delay. Li told the envoy: "All my men are innocent. I am the one who should be blamed. I will bear the brunt of all the charges on myself alone." When the envoy left, Li told his subordinate: "I have experienced many battles since I was enlisted. This time I thought of serving as a vanguard general in fighting the Huns. However, the commander-in-chief deployed my troops to travel a roundabout way so far away that I got lost. Now that I am over 60. How could I just wait to stand the trial and plead guilty?" After that he pulled out his sword and committed suicide. When his men heard about this, they all shed tears for him. Even civilians far and wide felt a great sadness about his death.

Historian Sima Qian, also a great man of letters in his day, wrote a sympathetic account of Li Guang's life story in his *Records of the Historian*. He concluded his essay with the following statements: "I've met general Li Guang myself. He is sincere and as unsophisticated as a man from the countryside. He is not an eloquent man. However, after he died, those who knew him well and those who did not know him so well felt sad about it. His honest character outshone all the eloquent officials. There is a folk saying that goes like this: 'By means of its beautiful flowers and sweet fruit, the peach and plum trees attract people, without saying a word, people are drawn to them so that worn paths lie beneath them.' These words are simple, yet full of meaning."

The proverb "the peach and the plum do not speak, yet a path is worn beneath them" stems from this story. It is now a figure of speech which means that a man of true worth attracts admiration. So long as one is sincere and works diligently, one is sure to win the praise of men.

蚍 蜉 撼 大 树 可 笑 不 自 量
pí　fú　hàn　dà　shù　kě　xiào　bú　zì　liàng

It is ridiculous for an ant
to try to topple a giant tree

唐朝时，著名的文学家韩愈在文学创作方面取得了巨大的成就。他的散文为世人所推崇，被列为唐宋散文八大家之首。他的诗歌也写得很好，注重抒发真情实感，风格古朴苍劲，气势雄健。韩愈能成为一代文豪，是与他虚心向前人学习分不开的。他生平最爱读李白、杜甫的诗，从中吸取了不少创作营养。李白、杜甫去世后，有一些狂妄自大的人对李、杜诗文恶意诽谤、诋毁。韩愈得知后，十分气愤，马上写诗给予痛击。他在给他的学生张籍的一首诗中写道：

李杜文章在，光焰万丈长。

不知群儿愚，那用故谤伤？

蚍蜉*撼大树，可笑不自量！

这几句诗的意思是：李白、杜甫的诗文流传于世，放射出万丈光芒。哪知一群愚妄无知的小儿，竟然无端对他们诽谤、伤害。这就像蚂蚁想摇动参天大树，太可笑，太不自量了！

后来，"蚍蜉撼大树，可笑不自量"两句诗流传下来并被人们用作谚语，用以比喻力量微小，却不自量力，妄图动摇强大的事物。

*蚍蜉：大蚂蚁。

During the Tang Dynasty, Han Yu, a noted writer, achieved great success in his literary career. His essays are held in the highest esteem by the general populace and he has been ranked as one of the top eight essayists of the Tang and Song dynasties. He was also very good at writing poems. His poems are characterized by liveliness, an aura of primitive simplicity, heartfelt sincerity, and imposing grandeur. Han's prodigious literary success cannot be explained apart from his modest attitude towards learning from his predecessors. He loved to read poems by Li Bai and Du Fu, drawing much literary inspiration from them. After the death of Li and Du, some arrogant people slandered and defamed their poems. When Han learned of this, he became irate and immediately wrote some poems to counter their attacks. In a poem dedicated to his disciple Zhang Ji, he wrote:

> Brilliance of poems and essays by Li and Du spread far and
>   wide,
> Yet a group of ignorant little men purposely attempt to
>   slander and harm;
> How laughable they are! Just like some ants attempting to
>   topple a giant tree!

Later, the last two lines were passed down as a proverb to describe those who overrate themselves in attempting to topple something or someone of true greatness.

倒 持 干 戈　授 人 以 柄

dào　chí　gān　gē　　shòu　rén　yǐ　bǐng

Holding a weapon upside down is like giving the handle to others to attack oneself

公元前 607 年二月，郑国发兵攻打宋国。宋国大夫华元、乐吕领兵抵御。

一场激战开始了，郑国军队呼喊着冲杀过来。宋军首领华元把手一挥，将士们也呼喊着迎了上去。跑在最前边的是宋国的名将狂狡。他使着一根长戟，挥舞起来，势如猛虎；一阵刺杀之后，已有十几名兵士死在他手下。这时郑军中一员战将向他冲来，狂狡挺戟相迎。两个人斗了十几个回合，郑将渐渐支持不住，边战边退。狂狡紧追不舍，把对手逼到一口枯井边。郑将一下子跳进井里，狂狡哈哈大笑，对着井中喊道："你投不投降，不投降我这就刺死你。"郑将哀求说："我投降，请你用戟柄把我拉出来。"狂狡不加思索，倒持长戟，把戟柄递给郑将。郑将抓住戟柄，被拉了上来。不料他刚一出井口，冷不防用力一拉，一下子把戟夺了过来，并趁势刺向狂狡，狂狡这才后悔自己做了件蠢事，但为时已晚，手中没有武器，只好乖乖做了俘虏。

根据这个故事，后人引申出"倒持干戈*，授人以柄"这句谚语。比喻无意中为敌创造机会，自己害了自己。

*干和戈是古时常用的两种兵器，此处泛指兵器。

In February 607 B.C., the State of Zheng sent troops to attack the State of Song, and met with the resistance of the troops led by Hua Yuan and Le Lu.

A fierce battle ensued. With loud cries, the Zheng soldiers charged forward the enemy, while Song soldiers defended their territory courageously under the command of general Hua Yuan. Kuang Jiao, a Song general, took the lead. Wielding a long halberd, the tiger-like Kuang Jiao knocked down Zheng soldiers row after row, striking terror in the hearts of Zheng soldiers. Suddenly he saw a general from the enemy camp charged towards him. After a dozen or so rounds, the Zheng general gradually could not hold out and began retreating while still fighting. Kuang Jiao followed him doggedly, finally cornering him by an old dried well. The Zheng general jumped into the well. Kuang Jiao laughed heartily: "Surrender or I will kill you!" The Zheng general implored: "I surrender. I surrender. Please pull me out by the handle of your halberd." Without thinking, Kuang Jiao turned his halberd upside down and gave the handle to the one in the well to pull him out. Completely to Jiao's surprise, immediately after the man was helped out of the well, he seized the halberd from Kuang and bayoneted him with it. It was then that Kuang Jiao regretted the foolish thing he had done. But it was too late. Now with no weapon in his hand, all he could do was give himself up as a prisoner of war.

The saying "holding a weapon upside down is like giving the handle to others to attack oneself" came from this story. It is used nowadays metaphorically to mean unconsciously providing an opportunity for one's enemy will end up in harming oneself.

射 人 先 射 马 擒 贼 先 擒 王

shè rén xiān shè mǎ qín zéi xiān qín wáng

To shoot a man, first shoot his horse; capture the chief to beat his force

杜甫是唐代伟大的诗人,生活在唐朝由盛到衰的转折时期。杜甫一生饱受流离颠沛之苦,际遇极为坎坷。但是他没有因为个人的不幸而消沉,而是把个人的痛苦与国家命运、时代脉搏紧密联系在一起,写下了大量同情人民疾苦,反映社会现实的诗篇。天宝年间,西北边境的回纥、吐蕃等地的贵族统治者发兵入侵。唐王朝征集大批军队前往讨伐。杜甫得知这一消息,感到这场战争又将造成人力、物力上的很大牺牲与损失。他反对对外屈辱妥协,但也反对大肆杀伐,反对劳民伤财的扩边战争。为了表达这种思想,他接连写了一组诗共九首,称《前出塞》。其中第六首诗这样写道:

挽弓当挽强,用箭当用长。
射人先射马,擒贼先擒王。
杀人亦有限,立国自有疆。
苟能制侵陵,岂在多杀伤。

诗的大意是:拉弓理应选硬弓,射箭还是用长箭。射人不如先射杀他的战马,打败敌军最好先擒拿他们的首领。杀人应该有个限度,中国和外族原是有一定的封疆国界。只要能够制止侵略，又何必一定要多多地杀伤人的性命呢？

后来人们引用"射人先射马，擒贼先擒王"比喻打击敌人要先打击为首的敌人，办事情要先抓住关键问题。

Du Fu, a great poet of China, lived during the period when the Tang Dynasty was falling from the zenith of its power and prosperity. He lived a solitary wanderer's life and had his fill of distress and poverty, yet he never allowed personal misfortunes to succumb himself. By relating his own adversity with the destiny of the state and the pulse of the times, he wrote a great number of poems which reflected the sufferings of the common people. During the reign of Emperor Xuan Zong, the aristocratic Tubo and Ouigour rulers in the northwest lead an invasion against the Tang Dynasty. The emperor recruited a large army to suppress the invaders. When Du Fu heard about this, he perceived the war would result in heavy casualties and great losses of state property. Du Fu was opposed to compromise with the enemy on humiliating terms, yet at the same time, he was also against wanton destruction of lives and the boundary-expansion war which exhausted the people and drained the treasury. He expressed these thoughts in a series of poems, consisting of nine pieces, entitled *Song of the Frontiers*. The sixth stanza reads,

The bow you carry should be strong;
The arrow you use should be long.
To shoot a man, first shoot his horse;
Capture the chief to beat his force.
Slaughter shan't go beyond its sphere;
Each state should have its own frontier.
If an invasion is repelled,
Why shed more blood unless compelled?*

Later, the proverb "to shoot a man, first shoot his horse; capture the chief to beat his force" was used to mean that when attacking the enemy, one should first attack the commander, when wanting to get something done, one should first address the most important problem.

---

* The English translation comes from *Song of the Immortals* by Xu Yuanzhong.

欲 速 则 不 达

yù   sù   ˆzé   bù   dá

More haste, less speed

孔子的学生子夏要到莒(jǔ)父(今山东省莒县境内)去做地方官。临行前，他专门去请教老师，询问到任后，自己怎样办理政务。孔子向他交代了应注意的一些事后，又叮咛道："无欲速，无见小利。 欲速，则不达;见小利，则大事不成。"意思是：做事不要单纯追求速度，不要贪图小利。单纯追求速度，不讲效果，反而达不到目的;只顾眼前小利，不讲长远利益，那就什么大事也做不成。子夏表示一定要按老师的教导去做，就告别孔子上任去了。

后来，"欲速则不达"作为谚语流传下来，被人们经常用来说明过于性急图快，反而适得其反，不能达到目的。

Zi Xia, one of Confucius' disciples, was getting ready to assume his new post as magistrate of Jufu (present-day Juxian County in Shandong Province). Before setting off for Jufu, he paid a special visit to his teacher to seek his advice on how to handle his new office. After telling him about some of the dos and don'ts, Confucius added, "Do not make haste, and do not covet petty gains. If you make haste you will miss your goal; if you covet petty gains, you will fail in bigger and more important matters." This sentence means: In doing things, do not just purely stress on speed or go after small gains. Just to emphasize speed and not to care about the effect can, adversely, cause you to miss your goal entirely. If one only cares about short-term petty gains and fails to consider long-term interests, he will never be able to do anything great. After Zi Xia expressed his determination to follow his teacher's instruction, he bade Confucius farewell and went to assume his new office.

Later, "more haste, less speed" was passed down as a proverb, which means that over-anxiety and hastiness often bring opposite results and defeat the purpose.

班 门 弄 斧

bān　mén　nòng　fǔ

Showing off one's skill
with the axe before Lu Ban

　　李白是唐代的伟大诗人，一生留下许多脍炙人口的诗篇，因而有"诗仙"之称。李白一生很不得意，六十一岁时，病逝于当涂（今安徽当涂）县令李阳冰家中。当涂县西北长江边上，有个风景壮丽的地方名叫采石矶，李白就被埋葬在那里。从此，采石矶便成为游览名胜。不少游人经过此处，都要前来凭吊一番，有的还在墓地题诗留名。

　　明朝万历年间，有个名叫梅之涣的读书人也来到采石矶，当他看到李白墓前写满了游人胡诌乱题的诗句，很是生气，于是就提笔写了一首《题李白墓》诗：

　　采石江边一堆土，李白诗名高千古，

　　来来往往一首诗，鲁班门前弄大斧。

　　诗中的鲁班又叫公输班（般），相传是春秋时鲁国人。他是我国古代著名的建筑工匠，一生中设计和制造了许多精巧的器具，为后人积累了大量的木工制作和建筑经验，所以民间木匠一直把他奉为"祖师"。由于鲁班超人的木工技能和他所处的祖师地位，人们常常把那些在行家面前显示自己本领的人的行为比作"鲁班门前弄大斧"，后来简化为"班门弄斧。"

Li Bai was a great Tang Dynasty poet who bequeathed to posterity a wealth of splendid poems. Hence the nickname, "Poet Immortal." But this poet had a very uneven life, and at the age of 61 he died of illness at the home of the magistrate of Dangtu County (in present Anhui Province). His remains were buried at the scenic Quarrier's Terrace on the Yangtse River in the northwest of Dangtu County. Because of its association with the great poet, the Quarrier's Terrrace became a place of historical interest. Many tourists have come to pay a visit to Li Bai's tomb and some of them have inscribed their poems and names on the stone tablet in front of the tomb.

During the reign of Emperor Shen Zong of the Ming Dynasty, a scholar named Mei Zhihuan came to visit the place. Seeing the tomb was covered by the graffiti of tourists, Mei was very angry and wrote a poem with the title called *Dedicated to Li Bai's Tomb*, which reads:

Under a pile of earth at the riverside quarry
Are buried the remains of Li Bai,
A great poet with everlasting fame.
Visitors have left one poem after another,
Not knowing they are just like showing off their skills
    with axe
Before Lu Ban the master carpenter.

Legend has it that the master carpenter mentioned in the poem, Lu Ban, also known as Gong Shuban, was from the State of Lu during the Spring and Autumn Period. He was the most famous architect of ancient China. Throughout his life he designed and built countless exquisite instruments, leaving behind a rich legacy of carpentry and architecture experience. Chinese carpenters have since dubbed him "the founder of carpentry." For this reason, a person who likes to display his skill in the presence of an expert is described as "showing off his axe skills before Lu Ban."

道 高 一 尺　魔 高 一 丈
dào　gāo　yì　chǐ　mó　gāo　yí　zhàng

As the Tao rises one foot, the demon rises ten feet

　　据明代吴承恩所著的《西游记》载，唐僧师徒四人往西天取经，一路上经历了千辛万苦。一天他们来到一座险峻的大山前面。远远望去，山凹中有一片楼台、房舍。唐僧在马上说："徒弟啊，咱们到山凹的住户那里化些斋饭，吃了再走。"孙悟空不同意："那边凶云漫漫，恶气纷纷，断不可去。请师父暂且下马，歇息一会，我去别处化些斋饭给您吃。"说着他扶唐僧下马，又用金箍棒在地上划了一道圈子，请唐僧、八戒、沙僧坐在中间；反复叮嘱他们不可出圈，否则将遭受毒害。

　　悟空去了一会儿，猪八戒对唐僧说："这里不藏风，不避冷，真要是有虎狼妖兽来了，这个圈子顶什么用？还是往前走走，找个地方避一避。"唐僧依了八戒的话，一齐走出圈外，不一会来到那楼台之处。八戒走了进去，房舍中却没有人，便顺手拿了床上的三件棉背心。不料，他和沙僧刚刚穿在身上，棉背心变作了绳索，把他俩倒背手捆了起来。师徒三人被妖魔轻而易举地捉入山洞中。

　　悟空化得斋饭回来，见没有了师父，心中大惊，急忙执着金箍棒寻到妖洞前。洞里魔王拿起一根一丈二尺长的点钢枪与悟空大战。两个战了五十回合，不分胜负。那妖魔急于取胜，喝令小妖助战，把悟空团团围住。悟空忍不住焦躁，把金箍棒往空中一抛，喝声"变"！即变作千百条铁棒，从空中落下来。妖魔见状，急忙从袖中取出一个亮灼灼白森森的圈子来，向空中抛去，叫声"着"！唿喇一下，把金箍棒套了进去。悟空手中没有了武器，慌忙打个筋斗逃命。这正是"道高一尺，魔高一丈"。悟空自恃本领高强，却败下阵来，无奈只好把太上老君请来才把妖魔降服。

"道高一尺，魔高一丈"原是佛家语。道指佛家修行达到的境界；魔，指破坏修行的恶魔，如烦恼、情欲、疑惑等。此语告诫修行者要警惕外界诸多影响修行的事物。这句话现在作为谚语使用，比喻反面力量超过正面力量，也泛指两方对立时，无论其中一方的手段多么高明，另一方总有压倒战胜对手的一着。

According to *Journey to the West* by Wu Cheng'en living during the Ming Dynasty (1368–1644), the Tang Priest (Tang Sanzang) and his three disciples went on a pilgrimage to the west for Buddhist scriptures. After undergoing countless hardships, they came to a terrible and dangerous mountain. From the distance, they spied a group of cottages in the vale. The Tang Priest said: "Let's collect some vegetarian food from the villagers. We can set off after we have something to eat." But the Monkey Sun Wukong did not agree: "There seems to be an ominous air over that mountain. We will be in danger if we go there. Master, please dismount and take a rest. Let me find the food somewhere else." Saying this, Monkey helped Sanzang off the horse, drew a big circle with his golden cudgel, and asked his master and two brothers to sit in the circle. Monkey told them again and again not to walk out of the circle. Otherwise they would suffer disaster.

After Monkey left, Pig said to his master: "This circle can shelter us from neither wind nor cold, if beasts or demons really come I doubt this circle will be of any help. Why shouldn't we keep going and find shelter for ourselves?" Sanzang followed Pig's words and walked out of the circle. After a while, they came to the cottages. When they went into one of the houses and found only three jackets on the bed, Sanzang and his two disciples took the jackets and put them on. Suddenly the jackets became ropes and tied them tightly up. Just as easily as this, Sanzang and his disciples were captured by a demon and thrown into a cave.

Coming back with the food, Monkey did not find his master and got frightened. In a hurry, Monkey carried his golden cudgel and found his way to the demon's cave. Wielding his iron staff, the demon fought 50 rounds with Monkey, but still there was no clear winner or loser. So the demon called his fellow demons for

216

help and surrounded Monkey. Monkey got impatient and tossed his cudgel into the sky, shouting "Change!" The cudgel turned into thousands of little cudgels and attacked the demon. The demon took out a shining ring and tossed it into the sky, shouting "Bingo!" In a flash, Monkey's cudgels were caught in the ring. With the loss of his weapon, Monkey was forced to run away. This is called "as the Dao rises one foot, the demon rises ten." Monkey counted on himself but was defeated. He had to turn to Lord Lao Zi to capture the demon.

The proverb "as the Dao rises one foot, the demon rises ten" was originally a Buddhist expression. Dao refers to the ultimate goal that all Buddhists strive for; the demon refers to such demonic spirit as libido, suspicion and vexation that undermines the ascetic's determination. This phrase admonished practicing Buddhists of the dangerous effects that outside world would have on their practice. Later it developed into a proverb, implying that the negative force surpasses the positive force, or that when two forces confront each other, no matter how strong one side is, the other side always has a way to crush it.

精 诚 所 至　金 石 为 开

jīng chéng suǒ zhì　jīn shí wéi kāi

Utmost sincerity can pierce
even metal and stone

　　古时候，楚国有一位著名的射箭能手叫熊渠子。 有一天夜里，他出门办事。 当他经过一片山林时，忽然望见前面不远的地方卧有一只老虎。 他吓出了一身冷汗，赶紧拉弓搭箭，对准老虎就射。可是那只老虎不动也不吼。 熊渠子感到奇怪，壮着胆子走过去一看，原来是一块像虎的大石头；再一看，他射出的那支箭整个儿钻进石头里去了。熊渠子简直不敢相信自己的眼睛，心想：我的气力再大也射不穿石头啊！他后退了几步，又拿起一支箭，开弓向石头射去。 只听"啪"的一声，箭却被弹了回来。熊渠子又连射几回，都是这样。他弄不明白是怎么回事，于是摇摇头，叹口气，继续赶路去了。

　　这件事很快传了开来。人们议论说，熊渠子所以能射开石头，是因为他当时心志专一，精力高度集中。

　　"精诚所至，金石为开"这个谚语就是从上面的故事演变而来的。人们常用以说明只要专心致志，下苦功夫，就能达到目的；有时也用来比喻诚心待人，可以产生意想不到的效果。

One night, the famous shooter of the State of Chu, Xiong Quzi, went out on an errand. When he passed by a wooded mountain he spotted a tiger lying ahead of him. Xiong, scared, broke out in a cold sweat. In haste he fit an arrow, pulled his bow, and shot at the tiger. But to his surprise, the tiger neither budged nor roared. Feeling that this was very strange, Xiong gathered up his courage and went over to take a closer look. The "tiger" turned out to be a large stone in the shape of a tiger, and the arrow he shot had penetrated the stone. Xiong could not believe his eyes, thinking to himself: no matter how strong I am, it is impossible for me to shoot through a stone. Backing a few steps, he fit another arrow, drew his bow and shot at the stone again. But this time the arrow bounced back. Xiong tried several more times but the same thing happened. Not understanding the reason, Xiong shook his head, sighed, and walked away.

Soon, this story spread quickly. People argued that it was Xiong's single-mindedness at that moment that caused the arrow to miraculously pierce through the stone. This story gave rise to the proverb "utmost sincerity can pierce even metal and stone," which means no difficulty is insurmountable if one sets his mind on it. It sometimes can mean that if one treats people with utmost sincerity, it may produce surprising results.

醉 翁 之 意 不 在 酒

zuì wēng zhī yì bú zài jiǔ

The old drinker's real interest
is not wine

欧阳修，字永叔，别号"醉翁"，是中国北宋时杰出的文学家、史学家。《醉翁亭记》是他的散文代表作，向来为世人所称颂。

《醉翁亭记》写于公元 1045 年，当时欧阳修受奸臣排挤，被朝廷贬官到滁州（今安徽滁州市）做太守。他来到滁州后，没有因官场失意而颓废不振，而是把自己的情怀寄托于山水之间。滁州城西南有一座风景秀丽的琅玡山。山中草木繁茂，泉水叮咚，百鸟鸣啭，花香清幽，景色十分优美。在山的半腰靠近潺潺流水的地方，有个亭子，为山中和尚智仙所建造，欧阳修给它起个名字叫"醉翁亭"。欧阳修经常带领一些宾客来这里，摆上几盘小菜，一面饮酒，一面与朋友谈天说地，赏玩琅玡风景，怡然自得，十分快乐。每次来到这里，欧阳修总是带着醉意而归。一方面是他确实饮了酒，一方面是美丽的山水令其陶醉。他在《醉翁亭记》中这样写道："太守与客来饮于此，饮少辄醉，……醉翁之意不在酒，在乎山水之间也。山水之乐，得之心而寓之酒也。"这段话的意思是：太守我与客人一起来这里饮酒，稍微饮一点就醉了。……醉翁的心思不在酒上，而是在美丽的山水间的风景上面。山水给我的乐趣，陶醉着我的心，我把它寄托在饮酒上了。

后来，"醉翁之意不在酒"作为谚语流传下来，为人们经常引用，用以比喻虽然这样说或这样做，但本意不在此，而在于其他方面；有时，也用作贬义，比喻别有用心，另有企图。

Ouyang Xiu, who styled himself as Yongshu, and was also known by the nicknamed "old drinker," was an outstanding historian and man of letters during the Northern Song Dynasty. *A Record of the Old Drinker's Pavilion* was one of his representative essays and has been praised from generation to generation.

The essay was written in 1045 when Ouyang Xiu was squeezed out of the emperor's palace by the crafty court officials and demoted to the post of magistrate of Chuzhou Prefecture (present-day Chuzhou, Anhui Province). After his arrival at Chuzhou, Ouyang Xiu, instead of taking his disappointed official career lying down, projected his feelings on the beautiful local landscape. The Langya Mountain in the southwest of the prefecture was a picturesque place with luxuriant woods, gurgling streams, chirping birds, and delicately fragrant flowers. A pavilion built by a monk stood by a brook half way up the mountain, Ouyang Xiu named it "Old Drinker's Pavilion." He often brought guests there, had a few some dishes laid out for them. Nursing a cup of wine while talking and appreciating the beautiful mountain scenery, Ouyang Xiu felt very happy and content. Climbing down the mountain, he would become a bit tipsy not only by the wine but also by the intoxicating scenery. In his famous essay he wrote: I came here to drink wine with my guests and we got drunk with just a little wine.... This old drunk's real interest was not in the wine, but in the gorgeous landscape. The landscape intoxicated me with delight so I expressed my happiness by drinking wine.

Later, "the old drinker's real interest is not wine" was passed down as a proverb to imply that one's words or actions actually hold an altogether different meaning. Sometimes this proverb has the negative meaning of having an ulterior motive.

燕 雀 安 知 鸿 鹄 之 志？
yàn què ān zhī hóng hú zhī zhì

How can a swallow know
the ambition of a swan?

秦末农民起义领袖陈胜年轻的时候，在富豪家当雇工。有一次，他和几个雇工在农田里干活。休息时，大伙你一言，我一语，发泄对贫困生活的不满。陈胜对这些人说："如果我们中间，将来有谁荣华富贵了，不要忘记我们这些穷伙伴啊！"有个雇工听后，笑着说："你这个给人家做工的，哪里会富贵呢！"陈胜听了，长叹一口气说："嗟乎！燕雀安知鸿鹄*之志哉！"

后来，陈胜领导了我国历史上第一次农民大起义，建立了农民革命政权。在群众的拥戴下，他做了陈王，实现了他要做一番大事业的雄心壮志。

根据这个故事，后人将"燕雀安知鸿鹄之志"作为谚语使用，比喻胸无大志的人，是不会了解英雄豪杰的志向和胸怀的。

*鸿鹄：中国古代对天鹅的称谓。

Chen Sheng was the leader of a peasant rebellion at the end of the Qin Dynasty. At a young age, Chen Sheng tilled the land with the other farmhands. During their rest times, they ventilated their grievances about their poverty-stricken lives. Chen Sheng said to his fellows: "If some day one of us became rich and famous he should not forget his poor friends!" One of the farmers heard this and laughed: "How is that possible? You are just a poor farmhand!" Hearing this, Chen Sheng sighed: "How can a swallow know the ambition of a swan?"

Later, Chen Sheng led the first peasant rebellion in Chinese history and established a peasant regime. With the support of the common people, he became the new king, realizing his great ambition.

This story gave rise to the proverb "how can a swallow know the ambition of a swan?" implying that people with no ambitions at all will not understand the aspiration of a heroic figure.

鞠 躬 尽 瘁 死 而 后 已

jū　gōng　jìn　cuì　sǐ　ér　hòu　yǐ

Bend one's body to a task
until one's dying day

公元 223 年，蜀汉皇帝刘备病死。临终前，他拉着丞相诸葛亮的手说："你的才能高出魏帝曹丕十倍，必能完成统一中国的大业。如果我儿刘禅可以辅佐，你就辅佐他；如果他低劣无能，你自可取而代之。"诸葛亮听后，痛哭流涕地说："我会忠心耿耿地辅助刘禅，一直到死。"

刘备死后，诸葛亮担起了辅助刘禅治理蜀国的重任。他事必躬亲，尽心尽责，很快使蜀国恢复了国力，逐渐强盛起来。为了完成刘备生前努力统一中国的愿望，他曾先后六次率领军队攻打魏国，争夺中原。公元 228 年，诸葛亮集结军队，出兵北伐。临出征前，他上表*（史称《后出师表》）皇上，一方面说明征讨的目的，一方面表白自己对蜀国忠诚的心迹。表中最后说："臣鞠躬尽力，死而后已，至于成败利钝，非臣之明所能逆睹也，"意思是：我一定小心谨慎，竭尽全力为蜀国效命，直到死了为止。至于是成功还是失败，那就不是我的能力所能预见的了。"

后来，此句演变为"鞠躬尽瘁，死而后已"表示呕心沥血竭尽全力，贡献出自己的一切。

*表：古代奏章的一种。

In 223, Liu Bei, emperor of the Kingdom of Shu died of illness. Upon his deathbed, Liu Bei held Prime Minister Zhuge Liang's hand and said: "You are ten times more intelligent than Cao Pi (emperor of the Kingdom of Wei). I am sure you can accomplish the cause of unifying China. If my son Liu Chan is a competent ruler, you should assist him in governing; but if he is an inferior and incompetent ruler you can replace him." Hearing this, Zhuge Liang wept bitterly and said: "I will assist Liu Chan loyally until the day I die."

After Liu Bei's death, Zhuge Liang took upon himself to assist Liu Chan in administering the state. He looked after even the most trivial affairs of the state. Because he put his whole heart and strength into governing the state, soon the kingdom was restored to its former position of power and became increasingly prosperous again. To realize Liu Bei's unrealized wish to unify China, Zhuge Liang led six expeditions on the Kingdom of Wei in a bid for the Central Plain. In 288, Zhuge Liang mustered his troops and launched the northern expedition. Before setting off, Zhuge Liang presented a memorial to the emperor, stating the purpose of the expedition and expressing his loyalty to the Kingdom of Shu. The last paragraph reads: "I will exert all my heart and strength to serve the Kingdom of Shu until the day I die. But whether I succeed or fail, I cannot predict."

Later, this sentence developed into "bend one's body to a task until one's dying day," meaning to work heart and soul to get something done.

覆 巢 之 下 无 完 卵

fù cháo zhī xià wú wán luǎn

No eggs stay intact under
an overturned nest

东汉末年，孔子的二十世孙孔融在朝中作官。孔融性格孤傲，好发直言，常常对曹操的举动、行为加以指责、嘲讽，因此曹操对他很恼火。有一次，曹操调遣大军，准备攻打刘备和孙权。孔融知道后，讥讽说："这是不讲道理的人去打讲道理的人，怎么能不失败呢？"有人把这话传给了曹操。曹操正愁抓不到惩治他的把柄，一听这话，便以诽谤朝廷，扰乱军心的罪名下令逮捕孔融，处以死刑。

孔融有两个孩子，一男一女。男孩九岁，女孩七岁。当孔融被抓的时候，他俩正在下棋；看看父亲被抓走，谁也没有动，依旧低头摆弄棋子。家人看到这样，以为他们不懂事，就说："你父亲就要被杀了，还不快去看看。"两个孩子听了，慢慢抬起头来说："我们离死也不远了，'安有巢毁而卵不破乎！'果然，不一会，曹操派人来抓兄妹俩。两个孩子一点也不害怕，从容不迫地走向刑场。

后来，人们就把"覆巢之下无完卵"当作谚语使用，比喻整体遭殃，个体也不能幸免。

Towards the end of the Eastern Han Dynasty, Kong Rong, a 20th generation descendant of Confucius, was an official in the court. A proud and aloof man who spoke frankly, he often criticized and satirized Cao Cao's behavior. Cao Cao was very angry with him. Once, Cao Cao dispatched army forces and prepared to attack Liu Bei and Sun Quan. Knowing about Cao Cao's plan, Kong Rong said sarcastically, "How could an unreasonable man defeat reasonable men? He is sure to fail." Somehow these words reached Cao Cao, who was looking for an excuse to punish Kong Rong. So he had Kong arrested on charges of slandering the court and disrupting the morale of the army and sentenced him to death.

Kong Rong had two young children, a nine-year-old boy and a seven-year-old girl. When they saw their father being arrested they were playing chess. Neither of them moved, and they kept playing. The servant saw this and, considering them to be insensitive to what was happening, told them: "Your father is going to be executed, why don't you go and have a look?" The two kids said: "We too will die soon. How can the eggs remain intact under an overturned nest?" And just as predicted, after a while, Cao Cao sent soldiers to arrest the two children. Showing the slightest fear, sister and brother made for the execution place.

Later, this story was summarized into the proverb "no eggs stay intact under an overturned nest," meaning if the whole suffers disaster, the parts will not be spared either.

人 无 害 虎 心 虎 无 伤 人 意

rén wú hài hǔ xīn hǔ wú shāng rén yì

**The tiger won't hurt you
if you don't hurt the tiger**

东晋时，有个名叫郭文的人，从小喜爱游览山水，常常一个人跑到深山密林中十多天不回家。长大后，他的这个喜好有增无减。待到父母死后，他辞家远游，踏遍名山大川，最后在吴兴余杭（今浙江余杭）的大辟山中深谷无人之处住了下来。当时这一带山区猛兽经常侵入村庄，危害乡民。可郭文在深山里一住就是十几年，从没有遇到危险。一次，有一只老虎跑到他的住处，不停地摇头摆尾，张开大口对着郭文。郭文感到奇怪，仔细一看，原来老虎嘴里卡着一根骨头，于是他伸手把骨头拔了出来，那老虎吼叫着跑开了；第二天竟叼着一头大鹿送到郭文的住处。

后来，郭文的事迹传到了京城。丞相王导派人把郭文接来，安置在皇帝狩猎用的御苑里。朝廷官员问郭文："猛兽害人，人人畏惧，先生就不怕吗？"郭文说："人无害兽之心，则兽亦不害人。"

后来"人无害兽之心，则兽亦不害人"演变为谚语"人无害虎心，虎无伤人意"，比喻人不犯我，我不犯人。

During the Eastern Jin Dynasty there was a man named Guo Wen, who loved to travel and would often stay in the forests and mountains by himself for ten days at a time. When he grew up, this roving propensity became an obsession. After his parents passed away, Guo bid farewell to his hometown, visited almost every famous mountain in the country and finally settled down in an unexplored valley in the Dapi Mountain in Yuhang County (present Yuhang of Zhejiang Province). The place was frequented by wild animals, which often attacked the villages and preyed on the people. Guo Wen lived in this area for more than ten years, but he never was in danger. One day a tiger ran over to Guo Wen's home. It kept shaking its head and wagging its tail, while opening its mouth wide towards Guo Wen. Guo thought this was very strange. At a close look, he discovered that there was a bone stuck in the tiger's throat. Guo took the bone out of the tiger's mouth, and the tiger ran away with a roar. The next day the tiger dragged a deer to Guo's abode.

Later the story reached the country's capital. Prime Minister Wang Dao sent for Guo Wen and installed him in the imperial hunting ground. One official asked Guo Wen: "Wild animals hurt people, and everybody is scared of them. How come Master Guo is not afraid?" Guo Wen answered: "If you have no intention of hurting the animal, then the animals won't hurt you."

Since then this sentence has developed into the proverb "the tiger won't hurt you if you don't hurt the tiger," meaning that I won't attack others if they don't attack me.

天 时 不 如 地 利
tiān shí bù rú dì lì

地 利 不 如 人 和
dì lì bù rú rén hé

The time isn't as important as the terrain;
the terrain isn't as important
as the unity of the people

　　战国时期，孟子的弟子公孙丑，特别喜欢向老师提一些发人深思的问题。有一次，他问孟子："老师，决定战争胜负的重要因素是什么?"孟子想了想，说："天时不如地利，地利不如人和。"接着孟子举了个例子说："比如有一座内城三里，外城七里的城池，敌人包围起来却不能取胜。敌人既来围攻，一定是挑选时日而得天时了，可是却无法取胜，这正说明天时不如地利好。又比如有另一座城池，它的城墙很高，护城河很深，士兵们的武器很锐利，粮草也充足。可是当敌人一来进攻，守军便不战自溃，弃城而逃，这又说明地利不如人和好。所以说，限制人民不必依靠国家的疆界，巩固国防不必凭借山河的险要，威服天下不必仗恃武力的强大。得道者多助；失道者寡助(得到正义的人，帮助他的就多；失掉正义的人，帮助他的就少)。

　　听了这番话，公孙丑更加佩服自己的老师了。

　　后来，"天时*不如地利**，地利不如人和***"作为一句谚语流传下来，人们用它来说明人心向背是成功的决定性因素，

232

远远比"天时"、"地利"重要；也用以说明搞好人际关系的重要性。

　　*天时：指适宜的时令、气候等条件。
　　**地利：指有利的地理条件。
　　***人和：指得人心，上下团结。

During the Warring States Period, there was a student of Mencius named Gongsun Chou. He liked to pose profound questions to his teacher. Once he asked Mencius: "What is the most important factor determining the outcome of a war?" After pondering over this question, Mencius answered: "The time isn't as important as the terrain, but the terrain isn't as important as the unity of the people. For example, the enemy can besiege a city with an inner part covering three square *li* and an outer part seven square *li* but cannot take the city. Since the enemy came to attack the city they must have decided that this is the proper time, yet they still can't take the city. This proves that time isn't as important as terrain. For another example, there is a city with a high wall and a deep moat, and the soldiers all have sharp weapons and sufficient food. But when the enemy came to attack, the soldiers all retreated without fighting, eventually running away and abandoning the city. This proves that the terrain isn't as important as the unity of the people. Therefore, the governor doesn't have to rely upon the country's boundary to limit the people, the terrain's strategic importance to reinforce defense, and military might to unify the country. Those who secure justice will get more support; those who lack justice will get little support." After hearing this, Gongsun Chou admired his teacher even more.

Later, the sentence "the time isn't as important as the terrain, but the terrain isn't as important as the unity of the people" was handed down as a proverb, implying that the unity and support of the people are the decisive factors for victory; they are much more important than time and terrain. This proverb is also used to point out the importance of establishing good relationships with the people.

不入虎穴 不得虎子

bú rù hǔ xué   bù dé hǔ zǐ

No way to catch the tiger's cub
without entering the lair

东汉初年，匈奴贵族的力量比较强大，征服和统治了曾是西汉辖属的西域（今甘肃西部及新疆一带）广大地区。匈奴贵族残酷地压迫西域各国人民，还不断到汉朝边境骚扰掳掠，对东汉政权造成很大威胁。为了彻底击溃匈奴，朝廷委派大将班超出使西域，联络那里的国家；以便共同对付匈奴。

班超率领三十六人的使团首先到了鄯善国（今新疆鄯善县）。起初，鄯善王对班超一行很热情，愿意建立友好邦交，可是不久又迟疑不决，态度也冷淡起来。这是怎么回事呢？

原来，这时匈奴也派来了使者，向鄯善王威逼利诱，施加压力。鄯善王慑于匈奴人的胁迫，不敢再亲近汉朝使者。

班超很快了解到这个情况，就把随行人员召集到一起，说："现在，匈奴人从中插手破坏，我们将被抓起来，那时我们不但完不成使命，恐怕连性命也难保了！"大家问："那怎么办呢？"班超说："不入虎穴，不得虎子！当今之计，只有乘夜攻入匈奴使者的营地，把他们消灭，才能完成使命。"

当夜。班超率兵偷袭了匈奴人的营地，将他们一举消灭。

第二天，班超向鄯善王讲明了事情的经过，并重申汉朝政府对鄯善国的诚意。鄯善王十分高兴，立即表示同意与汉朝建立永久友好关系。

后来，"不入虎穴，不得虎子"作为一句谚语流传下来，人们用它来比喻不深入险境，就不能获得成功，有时也用以比喻不经过艰苦实践，就不能正确认识事物。

At the beginning of the Eastern Han Dynasty, the Huns aristocrats grew increasingly powerful. They captured and ruled the wide Western Regions (including present-day Xinjiang Autonomous Region, west Gansu Province and part of Central Asia) that used to belong to the Western Han Dynasty. The Huns aristocrats ruthlessly suppressed the people living in the Western Regions, pillaged and looted those living on the Eastern Han border, and menaced the Eastern Han Kingdom. To crush the Huns power, the emperor commissioned Ban Chao as the envoy to the Western Regions to form an alliance with the states there against the Huns.

Leading an entourage of 36 men, Ban Chao first reached the state of Shanshan (present-day Shanshan County in Xinjiang). At first, the king of Shanshan showed great hospitality to Ban Chao and his party and expressed his willingness to establish friendly relations with them. But several days later, the king became hesitant and even cold to Ban Chao. How could this be?

It turned out that the Huns had also sent an envoy to Shanshan, using both threats and inducement to coerce the king of Shanshan. Fearing the pressure from Huns, the king of Shanshan no longer dared to be intimate with Han's envoys.

Ban Chao soon found out about this situation and called his men together: "Because of Huns interference we might get caught. In that case, we might fail to fulfil our mission, and our lives are in danger." "What should we do now?" asked his men. Ban Chao said: "How can you catch the tiger cub without entering the tiger's lair? What we can do now is to sneak into the Huns envoy's camp at night and take them by surprise. Only thus can we finish our task." That night Ban Chao and his men attacked the Huns campsite and wiped them out in one blow. The next day Ban Chao explained the whole thing to the king of Shanshan and reiterated the Han Kingdom's sincerity. The king agreed immediately to establish long-standing friendship with the Han Kingdom.

This story gave rise to the proverb "no way to catch the tiger cub without entering the tiger's lair," implying nothing ventured, nothing gained. If one does not enter into the heart of danger, one cannot attain success. It also means those who have not been tested by hardship cannot have a clear understanding of the issue.

不用空城计 退不了司马懿

bú yòng kòng chéng jì　　tuì bù liǎo sī mǎ yì

No way to repel Sima Yi
without the empty city ruse

中国古代四大名著之一，明代罗贯中所著的《三国演义》中记载了这样一个故事：

蜀国丞相诸葛亮率兵北伐魏国，因用人不当，丢掉了战略要地——街亭。诸葛亮感到取胜已不可能，就派遣几路兵力分别阻挡伏击魏军。待调遣人马停当，身边只剩下二千五百名兵士和一班文官。忽然有人飞马来报，说魏国大将司马懿率领十五万大军向这里涌来。诸葛亮走上城楼一看，只见尘土飞扬，魏军分两路杀来。于是连忙传下命令，把四面城门大开，每一个城门，由二十个军士扮作百姓，清扫街道。他同时告诫人们："如果魏兵来到，不可乱动。"他自己则带了两个书童坐在城楼上焚香弹琴。

魏军来到城下，见了如此情景，都不敢前进，急忙报告司马懿。司马懿立即下令停止进军，然后来到城下观望。果然看见诸葛亮端坐于城楼上，笑容满面，悠闲地弹琴；城门内外，有二十多个百姓，低头洒扫，旁若无人。司马懿看了，心中大疑，连忙传下军令火速撤退。他的儿子司马昭询问原因，司马懿说："诸葛亮平生谨慎，从不冒险，如今大开城门，必有埋伏，我如果进兵，必中其计。"于是将两部兵马全部撤去。

诸葛亮见魏军远去，禁不住拍手大笑。众官员询问其中缘故，诸葛亮说："我并非想要冒险，实在是不得已！"我们若弃城而逃，必不能跑远，最后还是要被司马懿捉住啊！"众人听了，无不佩服。

后来，人们根据这个故事概括出"不用空城计，退不了司马懿"这句谚语，用以比喻没有好办法，就不能克敌制胜。

· The following story is found in *The Romance of Three Kingdoms* by Luo Guanzhong of the Ming Dynasty, one of the four literary masterpieces of ancient China.

Prime Minister Zhuge Liang of the Kingdom of Shu led an attack on the Kingdom of Wei in the north. Because of his poor placement of personnel, the Shu army lost the strategic stronghold of Jieting. Assessing the hopelessness of regaining Jieting, Zhuge Liang dispatched several detachments to tackle the Wei army, leaving only 2,500 soldiers and a few civil officials with him. Suddenly a soldier showed up and reported that Wei's general Sima Yi, leading an army of 150,000, was quickly nearing the city. Walking up to the city tower, Zhuge Liang saw flying dust in the distance and the Wei's army closing in on them along two routes. Zhuge Liang hastily ordered that all the four city gates be opened, and twenty soldiers disguised as street sweepers be deployed at each gate. He warned his men not to panic when the enemy came, and sitting on the rostrum of the city tower with two servants he began playing a stringed instrument amidst the smoke of burning incense sticks.

As they drew near the city and saw this scene, the Wei army did not dare to advance and reported the situation to Sima Yi. Sima Yi ordered the troops to stop at once and personally went to the city wall to check out the situation. To his surprise, Zhuge Liang indeed was playing a stringed instrument and smiling leisurely on top of the gate tower, and below him about twenty civilians were sweeping the street as if nobody was around. Suspicion clouded Sima Yi's mind and he ordered the whole army to make a hasty retreat. His son Sima Zhao asked why and Sima Yi answered: "Zhuge Liang is a careful man and never takes risks. But today he opened every city gate so it must be a trap. If I attack I will for sure fall into his ambush." Just like this, both camps of the Wei troops retreated.

Seeing the withdrawal of the Wei's army, Zhuge Liang clapped his hands and laughed. When the officials asked why he laughed, Zhuge Liang said: "It was not that I wanted to take a risk. I really had no other choice. If we abandoned the city we surely would not have gotten very far before being caught by Sima Yi." At these words, admiration welled up in everybody's heart.

This story gave rise to the proverb "no way to repel Sima Yi without the empty city ruse," implying that it is impossible to defeat the enemy without a good stratagem.

机 不 可 失　时 不 再 来

jī　bù　kě　shī　　shí　bú　zài　lái

Opportunity knocks but once

韩信是汉高祖刘邦手下著名的大将。此人足智多谋，善于用兵，为汉朝的建立，立下了汗马功劳。

汉高祖四年（公元前203年），韩信打败了楚王项羽派出的军队，占领了楚军后方广大的地区，被刘邦封为齐王，名声大振。

当时，齐国有个叫蒯（kuǎi）通的人，看到韩信处于举足轻重的地位，便来劝说韩信背汉自立。他说："你先脱离刘邦"，与刘邦、项羽二人三分天下，然后再等待时机，各个击破，统一天下。"韩信说："这怎么可以呢？汉王一向待我不薄，我怎么能背叛他呢？"蒯通冷笑着：你以为忠心耿耿就可以得到好的报答吗？你现在功盖汉军，名振天下，居于人臣之位却有使人主担忧的威势，因此我深为你感到忧虑。"韩信不以为然。

两天后，蒯通又来劝韩信说："明智的人处事应该坚决果断。'夫功者难成而易败，时者难得而易失也。时乎时，不再来。'（意思是：做一件事要取得成功是很难的，而失败却很容易，要得到时机是很难的，而失掉却很容易。时机啊时机，一旦失去就不会再来了。）希望你仔细考虑，不要错过现在的有利时机。"

韩信听了，还是犹豫不决，不忍叛离汉王；又想到自己为刘邦出了那么大的力，他决不会加害自己，于是他拒绝了蒯通的建议。后来，韩信被刘邦之妻吕后以谋反的名义杀掉了。被杀之时，韩信仰天长叹说："我后悔当初不用蒯通之计，终究遇害！"

后来，人们从这个故事中概括出"机不可失，时不再来"的谚语，用以表示时机要紧紧抓住，不可错过。

Han Xin was a famous general who served under Liu Bang, emperor of the Western Han Dynasty. He was a man known for his strategic mind and excellent deployment of men. His heroic deeds on the battlefield contributed greatly to the establishment of the Western Han Dynasty.

In the fourth year of the Western Han Dynasty (203 B.C.), Han Xin defeated the army of the State of Chu and occupied its vast territory. Liu Bang crowned him as the new Duke Qi Wang and he became famous overnight.

At the time there was a man in the State of Qi named Kuai Tong. Observing Han Xin's pivotal position in the state, he came to persuade Han Xin to betray the Han and establish his own country. Kuai Tong said to Han Xin: "You'd better break away from Liu Bang and share the whole land with Liu Bang and Xiang Yu. Then you may wait for the opportunity to attack them one by one, so you can eventually unify China all by yourself." Han Xin said: "The emperor has always treated me well, how can I betray him?" Kuai Tong sneered at him: "Do you think you will be rewarded for your loyalty? Although you have contributed so much to the Han and won national fame, your position really poses a threat to your master. So I am really worried about you." But Han Xin didn't take his advice seriously.

Two days later, Kuai Tong persuaded Han Xin again: "A wise man should be resolute in handling matters. It is very difficult to succeed, but easy to fail; good opportunities are very hard to come by and very easy to lose. Don't let this opportunity slip, it may never come again! I hope you can think this over, please don't let go of this golden opportunity that you have now." But Han Xin was still hesitant for he could not bear the idea of betraying Liu Bang. He thought that after winning such big victory for the Han, Liu Bang surely would not hurt him. So he rejected

Kuai Tong's proposal. Later Liu Bang's wife had Han Xin killed under the pretext of political conspiracy. Before he was executed, Han Xin looked up at the sky and sighed heavily: "Oh! how I regret that I didn't follow Kuai Tong's advice! Now I am the one to suffer!"

This story gave rise to the proverb "opportunity knocks but once," meaning that one should never let a good opportunity slip through his fingers.

有眼不识荆山玉

yǒu yǎn bù shí jīng shān yù

Having eyes but not recognizing Jingshan jade

相传春秋时候，有个叫卞(biàn)和的楚国人，在荆山(在今湖北武当山东南)中得到一块璞玉，就捧着它去献给楚厉王。厉王很高兴，准备重重赏赐他。不料，朝中的一个玉匠却说："这不过是一块普通的石头，哪里是什么宝玉！"暴虐的厉王以为卞和欺骗自己，就叫人砍断了他的左脚，赶出京城。

　　几年后，楚厉王死了，武王继位。卞和又捧着那块璞玉去献给武王。武王请玉匠来鉴别，玉匠还说是石头，武王也认为卞和欺骗，就叫人砍断了他的右脚。

　　后来，楚武王死了，文王继位。卞和有心想再去进献，又怕遭到不幸。他越想越伤心，就抱着璞玉在荆山脚下痛哭。

　　楚文王听到这个消息，派人去问个究竟，卞和回答说："我并不是为失去双脚而悲伤，我痛心的是，珍贵的玉石反倒被当作普通的石头，忠诚的人却被说成骗子。"

　　楚文王知道真情后，就把卞和请进宫中，又吩咐玉匠治理那块璞玉，果然雕琢出一块晶莹剔透的宝玉。文王为表彰卞和的赤诚之心，就以他的名字为宝玉命名。

　　后来，人们根据这个故事概括出"有眼不识荆山玉"这句谚语。比喻不识好人或有才能的人，或者不识名贵的物品。

Legend has it that during the Spring and Autumn Period, there was a man from the State of Chu named Bian He who found a rough piece of jade in Jingshan Mountain (present-day southeast Wudang Mountain of Hubei Province) and presented it to Duke Li Wang of Chu. Duke Li Wang was very happy and decided to reward him handsomely. But a jade carver in the court said: "This is just a piece of ordinary stone, not a piece of precious jade at all!" The tyrannous duke thought that Bian He was cheating and punished him by chopping off his left foot and chasing him out of the capital.

Several years later Duke Li Wang died. Bian He presented the same piece of jade to his successor, Duke Wu Wang, who asked the same jade carver to judge it. When the jade carver told him that it was a piece of stone, Duke Wu Wang ordered that Bian He's right foot be cut on charge of fraud.

After Duke Wu Wang died, he was succeeded by Duke Wen Wang. Bian He wanted to present the jade but was afraid to be punished again. The more he thought, the sadder he became, and he wept at the foot of the Jingshan Mountain. Hearing this news, Duke Wen Wang sent people to ask Bian for the reason. Bian He answered: "It is not because I lost my feet that I cried. What makes me sad is that the precious stone is taken as a common stone, and I, an honest man, am considered as a cheat." Knowing the truth, Duke Wen Wang invited Bian He into the palace and ordered a jade carver to polish the uncut piece of jade. As Bian claimed, it turned out to be a sparkling and translucent piece of precious jade. In order to command Bian He for his loyalty, Duke Wen Wang named this precious jade after Bian He.

This story gave rise to the proverb "having eyes but not recognizing Jingshan jade," referring to one who cannot appreciate or recognize a good man, good talent, or something precious.

三 顾 茅 庐

sān   gù   máo   lú

Three calls on the thatched cottage

东汉末年，军阀混战。几经争夺，曹操统一了北方，势力最大，孙权则继承父兄基业，占据江东。唯有刘备四处奔波，始终未能取得自己的一块地盘。长期的失败教训，使刘备懂得了人才对于成就大业的重要性。于是他开始四处求人才。当他听说隐居在卧龙岗（即隆中，今湖北襄阳西二十里）的诸葛亮，博才多学，精晓文韬武略时，便下决心请他出山，辅佐自己干一番事业。

一天，刘备带着礼物，与其结拜兄弟、得力助于关羽、张飞一起来到隆中诸葛亮所住的茅屋。不料诸葛亮不在家，刘备惆怅不已，只得回去。过了几天，刘备又与关、张二将冒着大风雪登门拜访，诸葛亮仍不在家。刘备无奈，便留下一封言辞恳切的信回去了。又过了些天，刘备一行人第三次来到隆中。当时正值诸葛亮在睡午觉，刘备让关、张二人守在门外，自己恭敬地站在床前等候。书童几次要喊醒诸葛亮，都被刘备制止了。直等到诸葛亮醒来，才施礼相见。

一番谈话后，刘备对诸葛亮的才识十分佩服，流着眼泪恳请他出山相助。诸葛亮见刘备真心实意相请，又确有一番抱负，就答应了。

根据这个故事，后人概括出"三顾茅庐"这条谚语，比喻真心诚意相请有能力的人，因而常作为请人时的客套语。

Towards the end of the Eastern Han Dynasty, China was in a period of political turmoil and war among warlords. After repeated struggles, Cao Cao unified the north and emerged as the strongest power; and Sun Quan inherited his father and brother's power over the area south of the Yangtse River. Only Liu Bei was forced to wander from place to place, since he had no land of his own. From his repeated failures, Liu Bei learned the importance of talent to his ambitious cause. So he began to look for talent all over the country. He heard of a man named Zhuge Liang who dwelled in seclusion in the Lying Dragon Hill (20 *li* west of Xiangyang County in Hubei Province). This man was known for his intelligence, strategic mind and extensive civil and military knowledge. Liu Bei thus decided to invite Zhuge Liang to leave his life of seclusion and assist him in his cause.

One day Liu Bei and his sworn brothers Guan Yu and Zhang Fei brought gifts to the thatched house of Zhuge Liang but found him absent. Liu Bei was very disappointed and all he could do was going back home. Several days later, braving winds and snow, the three of them went to visit Zhuge Liang again but Zhuge Liang was still not home. Having no other choice, Liu Bei left a letter expressing his earnest interest in Zhuge and left. Several days later, Liu Bei and his men came to Zhuge Liang's thatched house for the third time. When they arrived, Zhuge Liang was having a nap. Liu Bei asked his brothers to wait outside the house and he himself waited respectfully beside Zhuge Liang's bed. For two or three times Zhuge Liang's servant wanted to wake him up but was stopped by Liu Bei. Liu Bei waited patiently until Zhuge Liang woke. Their conversation filled Liu Bei with such admiration for Zhuge's ability and insight that, weeping, he asked him to leave his country abode and serve as his assistant. Impressed by Liu's sincerity and high aspirations, Zhuge Liang agreed to his request.

This story gave rise to the proverb "three calls on the thatched cottage," implying one's sincerity in enlisting the help of a talented man. This proverb is usually used as a polite formula when inviting people.

（京）新登字 136 号

图书在版编目（CIP）数据

轻松学谚语：中英对照/李庆军，丁华编著．
－北京：新世界出版社，1998.9 重印
ISBN 7－80005－374－1

Ⅰ．轻… Ⅱ．①李… ②丁…
Ⅲ．①对外汉语教学-语言读物②汉语-谚语-汉、英
Ⅳ．H195.5

策　　划：姜汉忠
责任编辑：宋　鹤
版面设计：李　辉

轻 松 学 谚 语

李庆军　丁华　编著

＊

新世界出版社出版

（北京百万庄路 24 号）

邮政编码　100037

发行部电话：68326645

新华书店　外文书店发行

北京外文印刷厂　印刷

1998 年（汉英）第一版　1998 年北京第二次印刷

850×1168 毫米 1/32 开本

ISBN 7-80005-374-1/G·089

定价：22.00 元